THE SYLVAC COMPANION

A COMPANION TO 'THE SYLVAC STORY'

BOOK II

THE SYLVAC COMPANION

More Information on the Products of

SHAW & COPESTAKE LTD.
SYLVAN WORKS,
LONGTON,
STOKE-on-TRENT

AND

THOMAS LAWRENCE (LONGTON) LTD.
FALCON WORKS,
LONGTON,
STOKE-on-TRENT

A COMPANION TO 'THE SYLVAC STORY'

BOOK II

Mr. Richard Hull
Partner and Managing Director of
Shaw & Copestake 1935–1977

CONTENTS

ACKNOWLEDGEMENTS

In compiling this information many people have helped with research. Particular mention and special thanks to Mrs. Violet Brown and family, Mr. M. Chapman, Mrs. H. Evans, Mrs. J. Hallsworth, Mr. M. Harris, Mrs. J. Holdsworth, Mr. G. Matthews, Portmeirion Potteries Ltd., Mr. E. Roy Taylor, Mr. D. Willis-Utting.

Grateful thanks to my husband Peter for his continued support with this project and his patient reading of all the written material.

Illustrations reproduced from the Pottery Gazette by courtesy of Tableware International.

Photographs from the Pottery Gazette taken by The British Museum Newspaper Library, Colindale Avenue, London NW9 5HE. Unless otherwise stated all photographs are taken by the Author.

Many thanks also to the following collectors, dealers and friends who have all made important contributions to this book. Mr. K.H. Bizzell, Mrs. L. Blakeman, Mrs. M. Blenkinsop, Ms. A. Bouillot, Mr. J. Brooks junior, Mrs. B. Burkett, Mrs. A.H. Bury, Mrs. L. Cammidge, Mrs. F. Carter, Mr. & Mrs. A.I. Chew, Mrs. S. Cheetham, Mrs. Colclough, Mrs. H. Cossey, Mr. J. Cox, Mrs. J. Cox-Rogers, Mrs. J. DeDonna, Mrs. L. DeDonna, Mr. M. Dore, Mrs. J. Dickinson, Mrs. M.A. Espley, Miss J. Etches, Mrs. G. Finch, Mrs. K. Farncombe, Mr. A. Felton, Mrs. S. Gardiner, Mr. & Mrs. G. Gibbon, W.H. Griffiths, Mr. N. Hardcastle, Mrs. C.M. Hatton, Mrs. C. Hazeldine, Mr. & Mrs. R.A. Heath, Mrs. A. Holtham, Mrs. S. Horrigan, Mr. J. Howard, Mr. L. Howe, Mrs. P. Howe, Mr. K.A. Huckstep, Mrs. J. Hulme, Mrs. I. Hylands, Mrs. E. Hyder, Mr. D. Jackman, Mrs. J. Kamping, Mr. P. Landon, Mr. B.S. Lees, Miss J. L'Epine-Smith, Mr. T. Mark, Mr. W. Marsden, Mr. K.W. McDonald, Mr. J. McClusky, Mrs. C.M. Milnes, Mrs. M. Mullard, Mrs. A. Newman, Mr. & Mrs. R. Newton, Mrs. G. Notman, Mr. R. Philips, Mr. & Mrs. J. Piper, F.M. Plant, Mr. D. Richards, Mr. J. Roberts, Mr. S. Sherwood, Mr. J.A. Shevels, Mrs. P. Sorrell, Mr. F.W. Speight, Mr. B. Stalley, Mrs. J. Sturdy, Mrs. J. Sumbler, Mrs. P. Thake, Mr. R. Thompson, Mr. & Mrs. R. Walker, Mr. A. Van der Woerd, Mr. & Mrs. G.A. Verbeek, Mrs. V. Wabe, and other collectors who have kindly assisted with this project.

Although every care has been taken to eliminate errors, the possibility always exists. Readers who have noticed any mistakes or who have additional information to offer are invited to contact the Author at Pottery Publications.

Published by Pottery Publications, 7 Merton Park Parade, Kingston Road, London SW19 3NT.

Typesetting by Southwell Press Limited, Camberley.
Printed by The City Press, Biddles Limited, Walnut Tree House, Woodbridge Park, Guildford, Surrey GU1 1DA.

February 1991.   ISBN 0 9514889 1 0

FOREWORD

by Malcolm Chapman – Ex Director of Shaw & Copestake Ltd.

Following on the undoubted success of her first book, Susan Verbeek has written this second book which seeks to give information on SylvaC products in much greater detail. This book is a tribute to her hard work and in depth enquiries into the history of Shaw & Copestake Ltd., and its products. It is a 'must' for collectors and everyone interested in SylvaC ware.

MALCOLM CHAPMAN
Longton, Stoke-on-Trent

INTRODUCTION

May I thank everyone who has written to me regarding my first book The SylvaC Story. You have been most complimentary and apparently found it an extremely helpful source of information. It has been very gratifying to receive your letters, and most of you have disregarded the grammatical and spelling errors of a literary novice, and concentrated on enjoying the content. I can't promise that my literary prowess has improved, but I hope you will find the contents of this second book just as informative.

Since The SylvaC Story was published a considerable amount of new information has been found, including catalogues, advertising material and SylvaC Bulletins, (the staff magazine of Shaw & Copestake). I requested further information from collectors, and the response has been quite overwhelming with many collectors writing and sending wonderful photographs of rare SylvaC pieces. I have been amazed at the trouble everyone has taken and the kindness shown. Detailed measurements and drawings have also been received, and some of the photographs have been reproduced in this book. I have endeavoured to reply to every letter promptly, answering queries and sending photocopies where possible, which has been quite an achievement. I hope that telephone enquiries have also been dealt with helpfully and efficiently. I now have a large collection of archive material and will be very pleased to help collectors with queries about SylvaC, so do not hesitate to get in touch, via the Pottery Publications address. A stamped addressed envelope for a reply would be appreciated.

Having received all these wonderful letters and met many collectors, I thought it would be a novel idea to ask a few to write about their collections and I have persuaded four fellow collectors to put pen to paper. You will recognise a kindred spirit when you read their fascinating stories.

As the products of the Shaw & Copestake factory were so vast, I have decided to concentrate on the SylvaC period from approximately 1930 to 1982, with short mention of the following years until 1989 when the factory was under different management. The earlier period, from the turn of the century, when they were producing ornate vases, dressing table sets, toiletware, clock sets etc., is being covered in a separate book called Shaw & Copestake, The Collectors Guide to early SylvaC by Anthony Van der Woerd. Mr. Van der Woerd has specialised in this period and made extensive researches into the early products of the company. Although I have co-operated with the author as far as possible, his book is an entirely independent enterprise and not connected with Pottery Publications.

Collecting Thomas Lawrence (Longton) Ltd, Falcon Ware products has become more popular, and I have included a chapter and photographs of the beautiful pieces they produced before they joined forces with Shaw & Copestake, in 1938.

This book contains a list of Shaw & Copestake and SylvaC mould numbers which were not known at the time The SylvaC Story was published, a larger register of numbers can be found in The SylvaC Story and it is advisable to have both books for a comprehensive guide to collecting SylvaC. The SylvaC Story, published by Pottery Publications in 1989, contains a more detailed history of the companies, information about directors, designers and employees, the main register of mould numbers, and examples of marks used by Shaw & Copestake Ltd and Thomas Lawrence (Longton) Ltd.

I have endeavoured to impart some of the information available to me at the time of writing, but it is impossible to have complete knowledge of all SylvaC produced. Sometimes a new item of information can alter ones perception of the subject, and this should always be borne in mind when reading these notes.

SUSAN JEAN VERBEEK

LIST OF ABBREVIATIONS

h	height	S/s	small size
l	length	M/s	medium size
d	diameter	L/s	large size
HP	hand painted	Ass. Cols.	Assorted Colours
TSS	The SylvaC Story	Cell	Cellulose
Reg. No.	Registered Design or pattern number		

Note beforehand:-

Numbers in a **bold** type indicate they are in the register at the back of this book. Other numbers can be found in The SylvaC Story.

Numbers with F in front are Falcon Ware rather than Old Shaw & Copestake.

HISTORICAL NOTES

SHAW & COPESTAKE LTD, SYLVAN WORKS, NORMACOT ROAD, LONGTON, STOKE-ON-TRENT

THE FACTORY

Shaw & Copestake was founded around the turn of the century by Mr. William Shaw and Mr. Copestake. Mr. Copestake's position was taken shortly after by Mr. Richard Hull senior, who died in September 1935. Mr. Richard Hull junior, who had joined the firm in 1924 became Mr. Shaws partner on the demise of his father, and the business became a limited company in 1936. On Mr. Shaws retirement in 1942 Mr. E.J. Dennis became a director.

In 1938, Mr. Hull and Mr. Dennis acquired the factory of Thomas Lawrence (Longton) Ltd., Falcon Works, Waterloo Street, Stoke-on-Trent, who used the trade name of Falcon Ware on their products. The two factories operated independently until 1957, when new premises were built on land opposite the old Shaw & Copestake factory and both companies moved into the new works. The two businesses were gradually fully merged by 1964, after which time no more products with the Falcon Ware mark were made.

In May 1982, Shaw & Copestake went into voluntary liquidation, the land, buildings, plant and equipment were purchased by the North Midlands Co-Operative Society, later known as the United Co-Operative Society, and leased to a workers Co-Operative Society known as Longton Ceramics. Eighteen months later the United Co-Operative Society took over the business which was run in the name of Crown Winsor.

In June 1989 the business was once again sold and known as Crown Winsor (Pottery) Ltd., this Company went into liquidation in November 1989, the factory and shop were finally closed in December 1989. During this time the new Chairman of the Company became very interested in the SylvaC collectors and had the idea of forming a Collectors Club from the factory. He also set up a small museum of rare pieces found at the works.

On learning a receiver had been installed at the factory I naturally wrote and telephoned expressing my concern that the archival material be saved and offered to purchase it, but received no reply. It has been rumoured everything went to the highest bidder, but we were not invited to take part or informed of any auction. Unfortunately none of this material has so far re-surfaced. What has happened to it? It would be tragic if it was all lost.

The following Spring the premises were bought by Portmeirion Potteries Ltd., and are now occupied by them. No production took place at the Sylvan Works for the whole of 1990, during which time extensive renovation and installation of new equipment took place. Production commenced at the Sylvan Works in January 1991, producing castware for their standard range of pottery.

During 1992 it is anticipated that the Sylvan Works will once again be producing some SylvaC Ware, from the blocks and cases which were on the site when Portmeirion Pottery Ltd. purchased the Works. Special training of staff in the art of hand painting pottery is taking place, as this is a new technique for the Company.

SYLVAC

The trade name SylvaC was not used by Shaw & Copestake until about 1935, when Mr. Richard Hull junior decided the firm needed a less cumbersome trade name customers would remember. Mr. Malcolm Chapman a former director remembers his old friend telling him how he devised the name: "*Being unable to use the name of the works Sylvan, which was already used by another pottery, he struck on the idea of simply changing the 'n' of Sylvan for a large 'C' for Copestake.*"

Some of the earlier products of Shaw & Copestake carried a 'Daisy' mark, and this symbol was slightly altered about 1935 to incorporate the new SylvaC name. (See page 161 of The SylvaC Companion for photographs). It was not used for long, and very soon SylvaC became impressed or incised on the base of most of the wares. Some pieces have a stamp mark under the glaze. Later, in the 1980s instead of the usual 'SylvaC' or 'SylvaC Ware' some pieces were marked 'SylvaCeramics'. I have seen only one item actually marked Shaw & Copestake, this was from the baby ware range.

There is a range of toilet ware impressed with the name 'Silvo', and another called 'Napier'. These were produced in the 1920s and have no accompanying mould number. The majority of early ware had numbers, but some only carried the 'Daisy' mark, very often only one piece in a set of toilet ware or dressing table ware had a 'Daisy', the other pieces were unmarked making them difficult to identify.

When Shaw & Copestake products were made in the Thomas Lawrence factory, they were usually stamped with the words SylvaC Ware in a slanting flowing style.

THOMAS LAWRENCE (LONGTON) LTD, FALCON WORKS, WATERLOO ROAD, LONGTON, STOKE-ON-TRENT

Although the Thomas Lawrence (Longton) Ltd. factory was producing Falcon Ware, and had its own numbering system and mark, some of the products were also stamped with the SylvaC Ware logo. These could either be Falcon Ware products stamped SylvaC, or the original SylvaC moulds used at the Thomas Lawrence factory during the war. Shaw & Copestake moved their production to the Falcon Works due to the 'concentration of industry' policy which applied during World War II.

The Thomas Lawrence factory used its own numbering system 1 to roughly 759, from about 1940. Consequently these numbers overlapped the original OLD Shaw & Copestake numbers dating from the early 1900s to about 1930. This means collectors are in constant danger of assuming a LOW Falcon Ware number is an EARLY Shaw & Copestake number. Although I have tried to explain this as clearly as possible in The SylvaC Story, collectors still have difficulty in grasping this fact. Especially as, at the time of publishing the first book not many of the old Shaw & Copestake numbers had been found. However many more old numbers have been collected and these now form part of a separate register at the back of this book.

MR. WILLIAM SHAW founder of Shaw & Copestake Limited

I was very intrigued to receive a letter one day from Mrs. Violet Brown, who actually knew Mr. & Mrs. William Shaw and their family. This was the first break through I had in tracing Mr. Shaws family as until then Mr. Shaw had been an enigma, no one would admit to knowing him well, this is Mrs. Brown's tale:
"*In 1912 when I was about six years old my father took in a stray dog, at that time he was in a business with a post office attached. Father saw that it was a pedigree dog, and reported it to the police. Apparently a reward of £5.00 was offered for the return of the dog, my father not wanting the £5.00 was given instead a large hamper of all kinds of crockery by Mr. William Shaw, to whom the dog belonged. The dog got lost when Mr. Shaw had been at a shoot some few miles away. The hamper contained among other items a set of three jugs with the 'Daisy' mark.*"

▲ 'Clovelly' the former home of Mr. William Shaw and family at Blythe Bridge, Stoke-on-Trent. It is now a Guest House, and manager Mr. William Marsden is standing in the doorway. Photograph taken in 1989 by Peter Lepino.

Tombstone in memory of Mr. William Shaw's dog ▶ 'Major Shaw' erected in 1922. It is still in the garden of Clovelly House. Photograph taken in 1989 by Peter Lepino.

Mrs. Brown later became well acquainted with the family for many years, and was able to tell me that Mr. & Mrs. Shaw and family had lived at a house called Clovelly, on the Uttoxeter Road, Blythe Bridge, which is now a guest house. The present owners very kindly showed us over the house and in the garden was a gravestone in memory of the very dog Mrs. Brown's father had found. The dog was called Major Shaw, and was obviously much loved by the Shaw family. On the headstone was engraved 'In Memory of Major Shaw – died Dec 28th 1922 – Aged 12 – Always good and faithful'.

An interesting aspect of this story is that the set of jugs given to Mrs. Brown's father in 1912 had the Shaw & Copestake 'Daisy' on the bases, which until now had been thought to date from 1925, when it was first mentioned in The Pottery Gazette. If this is correct the information on page 67 of The SylvaC Story regarding the dating of the 'Daisy' mark is suspect. But I would point out this new information has yet to be confirmed from another independent source.

During the course of their friendship Mrs. Brown received several gifts from the Shaw family, amongst which was a black cat and a vase for a wedding present, and for her 21st birthday a vase and bedroom clockset. She was also taken on a conducted tour of the Old Shaw & Copestake factory, which she still remembers well.

Unfortunately we have not been able to trace any member of the Shaw family willing to help us with our researches, and the hoped for old original catalogues have still not been found. But I am very grateful to Mrs. Brown who has endeavoured to trace the family, for this new and exciting information.

▲ The three jugs given to Mrs. Violet Brown's father in 1912. They have the Shaw & Copestake Daisy mark.

COLLECTING SYLVAC

An interesting aspect of collecting SylvaC is the continuing search for unknown pieces, which means we can all take part in the gradual process of recording the SylvaC products.

There have been quite a few comments lately at the high price of some SylvaC, which of course is inevitable as more collectors are now after the same items, but it is still possible to find the odd piece for a few pounds. I have to admit to being guilty of paying a high price for something I really covet, and ultimately it is up to the buyer to decide whether to pay the asking price or wait in the hope of seeing something more reasonable.

Several people have requested a price guide, which would be quite difficult given the number of pieces involved, the great variation found in prices, and the fact that it would virtually be out of date so quickly. I agree it might be helpful to have a very general guide to the value of certain items, but can only suggest you check out the dealers stalls for the latest trend in SylvaC prices.

There are now thousands of SylvaC collectors and numbers are growing all the time, including collectors in America, Australia and New Zealand who have all the popular SylvaC pieces in their possession.

SylvaC rabbits have recently become most collectable, making them very difficult to find. Large 10″ rabbits, number **1028**, are quite scarce and commanding high prices, especially in the rarer colours. Many people collect rabbits of every size and colour, and are reluctant to part with them once they have eventually been found. Green and fawn matt glazes are more frequently seen, most rare are blue rabbits, also much sought after are pink and yellow examples. Many other potteries made rabbits, and I would stress the importance when looking for a SylvaC rabbit of checking that the mould number is on the base, even if only part of it can be seen.

SylvaC dogs are also much collected and loved, there are over two hundred different models to choose from, with colour variations, which gives one plenty of scope. The prices vary from a few pounds to nearly one hundred pounds for large or rare models. Please be very careful when buying unmarked or un-numbered dogs, as there are many green matt dogs around which are not SylvaC, some were made by Price Bros. (Burslem) Ltd., and others by H.A. Wain & Sons Ltd., Longton, who used the trade name 'Melba Ware'. The Wade Heath Company Limited, also produced many animals, including dogs, in similar styles and colours to SylvaC dogs.

Dogs produced in later years at the Sylvan Works were generally hand painted in natural colours, sometimes the numbers are difficult to read. I have endeavoured to photograph most of these in order to help you identify them as they are now becoming very collectable.

Other SylvaC animals and birds are very worthwhile and interesting to collect and many different species were modelled. They tend to be expensive as they were not produced in large quantities. Some models such as the Prestige range, are of a classical design, while others are comical or characterisations of animals. These were probably originally intended for children. If found in good condition the colourful cellulose finish which is unglazed, can be very collectable.

Some collectors are now interested in the old Shaw & Copestake products dating from the turn of the century, and if you like the highly decorated and ornate pieces you will find these very pleasing. The cheaper range of the market at that time was the cellulose ware and some very colourful vases, clock sets, bowls and plant pots have been found in this range. This subject is covered in depth in a separate book, by another author.

The Shaw & Copestake figures are also very collectable and a good investment. There are of course many pieces still to be recorded and I hope if you find any rare examples you will let me know. The latest discovery has been a Goblin/Genie sitting on a grassy mound, number **842**.

Since I wrote about the rarity of some items the market has suddenly become flooded with them, as in the case of the Harrods doorman character jug and Mr. SylvaC ashtray.

The doorman, number **4497**, was originally only supplied to Harrods and was thought to contain tea. It was rarely seen before The SylvaC Story was published in 1989. Mr. George Matthews who made the original model in 1981 was sent photographs of the doorman from Harrods, to model from, to make an authentic likeness. I was very puzzled to see number **4497** marked Carlton Ware, and it transpires the original mould was sold to them. Some of the jugs have the word Harrods highlighted in gold and a red rim to the hat, others do not. I have seen many marked Carlton Ware, the last one was priced sixty-five pounds and described as SylvaC/Carlton Ware which I suppose is a fair description. The Carlton Ware factory was closed in 1989, and the Harrods doormen were sold in quite large quantities at the closure sale. I have yet to find a genuine SylvaC marked Harrods doorman.

Although the Carlton Ware factory closed down, some of the moulds and the Carlton Ware name were purchased by Mr. John McCluskey who still produces some of the pieces at Grosvenor Ceramic Hardware Ltd., Emerald Way, Stone Business Park, Stone, Staffordshire. The Harrods doorman is not amongst them.

The Mr. SylvaC advertising ashtray, number **3542**, was made originally for dealers or shops to advertise SylvaC in 1964, about six hundred were produced. These have been re-issued recently, they were made from the original mould at the beginning of 1990, and are not the ashtrays made for dealers in 1964 which had FOR QUALITY AND VALUE on the front in gold. Prior to Pottery Publication's book launch at the SylvaC factory a small number of Mr. SylvaC ashtrays were found in the store room in an unpainted condition. We expressed interest in these and the Chairman of the then company thought it a good idea to paint them and offer them for sale in the factory shop ready for the book launch at twenty-five pounds each. They were painted in identical colours to the original ashtray, black and white, with the gold lettering omitted. I was told originally twenty or thirty had been found, but the supply seemed to be endless, and I think it possible the mould was found and more produced.

A circular letter was sent out after the closure of Crown Winsor (Pottery) Ltd, on 12th January 1990, by someone previously connected with the pottery, offering Mr. SylvaC ashtrays to collectors at forty-five pounds each. They were to be a limited edition, and made to order only. The letter was signed by the Club Secretary of the yet to be formed SylvaC Collectors Club, (not to be confused with The SylvaC Collectors Circle). It seems this venture was a failure and the remaining ashtrays were eventually sold to a SylvaC dealer.

The ashtrays are quite authentic in that they were made from the original mould and at the Sylvan Works, and it is quite a nice piece to have in a SylvaC collection. They can be found at antique fairs for prices ranging between thirty-five and two hundred pounds. I do not know exactly how many were finally produced, or if they will be produced again in the future, but they are certainly not as rare as some dealers would have you believe. Please refer to the Historical Notes for more information regarding the factory.

Many people collect SylvaC vases and jugs, which is a vast subject to cover. The green/fawn mottled or blended colours are most popular, and many thanks to collectors who have sent lovely photographs of beautifully displayed vases and jugs in the most subtle of colours, they make a very tasteful show in any cabinet. It is certainly more stunning to keep to one colour when displaying these items, and collectors have gone to enormous lengths to photograph their collections.

A popular display in kitchens is the pre-war tableware in green, blue and fawn matt glazes, once again the photographs of such displays have been remarkable. The kitchen is also the place for showing off the face pots, such as the onion, coleslaw, chutney bowls etc. many people collect these and they can still be picked up for a reasonable amount. They are more effective if displayed in one colourful group and make quite a focal point in the kitchen.

SylvaC is well known for novelty ware and fancies, and they dreamt up some weird and wonderful creations, which are well worth collecting, when you can find them. The SylvaC advertising and promotional ware is interesting but not too easy to find as it usually went directly to the Company or Society who ordered them, not to retail shops.

Fortunately SylvaC made items for each area of the home, which means you can have a display in every room. Pink floral dressing table sets for the bedroom, plenty of nursery ware, pipe holders and ashtrays for Dad, and swans and ducks for the bathroom. In fact the SylvaC ranges cover every aspect of life from the elegant, fashionable, nostalgic, amusing, useful, essential things in life to the quaint, unusual and sometimes dare I say, tasteless. But even the objects that perhaps you or I find a little 'out of the ordinary', someone else will absolutely love. It was suggested I ran a competition for the ugliest piece of SylvaC ever seen!

Many people are now collecting the early Falcon Ware produced before the merger with Shaw & Copestake. This was made by Thomas Lawrence, Falcon Works, Waterloo Street, Longton, Stoke-on-Trent, later to become Thomas Lawrence (Longton) Ltd. It does tend to be expensive but is of good quality, beautifully decorated and a sound investment. Once again, as with the early Shaw & Copestake, information is difficult to come by as no pre-war records of Falcon Ware products have yet been found.

All in all the collecting of SylvaC is on the increase, and many people are becoming fascinated by the subject. I hope this second book will enable you to identify more SylvaC to add to your collections.

▲ Harrods Doorman character jug number 4497 4½″ high. Photograph by Peter Lepino.

▲ This Mr. SylvaC ashtray was for sale in the SylvaC Factory Shop in 1989. You will notice the absence of the words 'For Quality and Value' on the front. Number 3542 8″ high. Photograph by Peter Lepino.

DOGS

During the last year quite a few unusual SylvaC dogs have been found, the earliest one is a large Airdale terrier attached to a vase. The dog is numbered **743**, the vase is separately numbered **827**, OLD Shaw & Copestake numbers, it is 7″ high and 9″ long. Possibly the two items were also used separately. The example I have in my collection has a cellulose finish which is constantly flaking off. The colour is best described as ginger and black, the numbers are very clearly impressed on the base, giving no rise to think it could be anything but Shaw & Copestake, but as it was made before the SylvaC trademark was used, has no SylvaC or Shaw & Copestake mark. As the number of the dog is **743**, I would think it was first produced in the mid to late 1920s, and up until the time of writing is the first known dog produced by Shaw & Copestake.

Dog number **1044** is a bulldog very much in the image of 'Bonzo' the comic strip cartoon dog. It is 8½″h and has a cellulose finish, the example found is in good condition in cream, with black ears, mouth and nose, yellow and black eyes, and a red tongue. It has a bow around its neck, which is also cream. The original price of 1/11½d is still written on the base in pencil. It was probably produced during the early 1930s.

Dog number **1117**, best described as a mongrel, is 7″h, a very bright orange coloured cellulose glaze, has green and black eyes, and a black nose. This one is priced on the base in pencil at 2/6d, and was also probably pre-war. He is a short stubby dog, with a large head and big sticking up ears.

No doubt these dogs were produced in a wide range of colours and finishes, as well as the ones mentioned above. Also please remember the dates given everywhere in this book are the possible FIRST production dates, or making of the original block and case for the mould, the item could have been made for many years following that date.

I have recently borrowed a pre-war Shaw & Copestake catalogue, from which I have learnt, and I am sure dog collectors will be interested to know this, that the little 'dog with bow' number **1119** is called 'DAISY' dog.

The small dog, number **1120**, 3¾″h has managed to elude me so far, but other collectors have managed to find this little chap in blue, green and fawn matt colours. I have hopes of adding him to my collection in the not too distant future. However I have been able to borrow him from his owner for a photographic session. He is very small and has what one would call a 'hang dog' expression probably as the result of a dressing down from his master.

A wonderful find by a collector has been an Alsatian type dog, number **1203**, 9″h. This is very sensational and unusual as the features on the face have not been painted. It has a green matt finish, a sphinx-like look to it, as if guarding an Egyptian tomb, and is in perfect condition. So far as I know, this is the only one to have been found. The owner has kindly lent a photograph for reproduction in this book. I haven't yet received any information about dog 1202, which is described in the Mould Makers Register as an Alsatian, and it may be a similar design to **1203** in a different size. There has been no information about 1204 which could also be in the same series.

It is nice to know there are four sizes of begging Joeys, **1191** 5″ high, **1192** 6″h, **1193** 8″h and **1194** 9½″h. They have been found in a variety of colours, including a very nicely decorated cellulose cream, black and orange, and also all the usual matt colours. These were produced before World War II, and although the smallest, number **1191**, has been documented up to 1965 the other sizes were probably shorter runs, in fact they are only shown in the 1930s catalogue and do not appear in any later brochures.

Several collectors have found the dog sitting with right paw raised, number **1475** 7¾″h, also the larger version **1476** which is about 11″h, no one has been able to identify which breed this dog is, but it slightly resembles a West Highland Terrier. The colours so far have been cream/brown, fawn, and green, matt finish, but no doubt they were produced in other colours as well. It is possible there was a range of three, if not more, but I have no further information at this time. It is beautifully modelled with very good detail, and a really lovely dog to add to your collection.

Quite a recent find has been puppy number **1647** 3½″h, this is an interesting piece, as it obviously partners puppy number **1646**, the playing puppy with his bottom in the air, and big eyes and eyelashes. Number **1647** is very similar but is sitting with his head slightly down and to one side, his eyes are closed and he adopts a coy attitude, he also has long eyelashes. Whereas puppy number **1646** is frequently seen, his friend number **1647** is quite rare, presumably it was not produced in such vast quantities. They both have a dimpled effect on the body.

A recent letter from a collector in Burnley, has prompted me to tell you about the two un-numbered poodles called Toby and Chum. They are in a similar style to poodle number 3174, but 1¼″ shorter. They carry their names on discs around their necks, and are usually seen in the cream lustre colour.

Also worth a mention are two spaniels, one holding a slipper in its mouth, and one a pipe, both look expectantly at their invisible master obviously waiting for a word of praise. The spaniel with the slipper is number 3827 5″h, he is very nicely modelled and decorated with plenty of detail, even having a flower on the slipper. The spaniel with the pipe has a number I cannot decipher and I have not been able to trace it in the register, but it is marked SylvaC. It is of the same era as number 3827, and very similar in style.

Some new information from a collector, and confirmed by ex Director of Shaw & Copestake, Mr. Malcolm Chapman, about plain white cats and dogs. Dogs numbers 2938, 2950 and 2951, with long faces, and three sizes of terrier dogs numbers 1378, 1379 and 1380, also cats numbers **1086** and **1087** were produced in plain white with no decoration, for the Dutch market. Look out for these on your next trip to Holland.

Portmeirion Potteries Ltd., had some SylvaC dogs for sale in their Factory Shop at the Sylvan Works in 1990 in a plain transparent glaze. These were items which were left on site by the previous owners, Crown Winsor (Pottery) Ltd., and fired to biscuit only. Portmeirion glazed some of these items as a way of commissioning new glazing and firing equipment, and sold them for one pound each in the Factory Shop. Portmeirion Potteries may produce some SylvaC Ware in 1992, using the moulds which are now in their possession. (Refer to Historical Notes.)

SylvaC dogs are very highly prized by collectors, some of whom go to enormous lengths to buy a particularly desired model. They can sometimes be found reasonably priced at boot fairs and bric-a-brac markets, especially if unmarked and the seller is not 'up' in SylvaC Ware. But some of the larger or rarer models are now being priced at around one hundred pounds each, and no doubt there will be a steady increase in the value. The SylvaC dogs are hopefully to be mentioned in the May 1991 issue of the magazine Homes and Gardens by Deborah Stratton, which will possibly make them even more sought after. There are, no doubt, many dogs not on the SylvaC register so please keep looking for new examples.

Sealyham 5323
190mm (7½") *long*

Old English Sheepdog 5322
178mm (7") *long*

Pyrennean Mountain Dog 5324
255mm (10") *long*

Golden Cocker Spaniel 5076
190mm (7¾") *long*

Springer Spaniel 5434
203mm (8") *long*
Black & White or Brown & White

English Setter 5170
235mm (9¼") *long*

Great Dane 5258
225mm (8⅞") *long*

Whippet 5260
153mm (6") *long*

Schnauzer 5259
176mm (7") *long*

▲ Hand decorated Supreme Dogs. Page from SylvaC catalogue c.1980.

Chihuahua 5319
145mm (5¾") *High*

Corgi 5321
170mm (6¾") *Long*

Dachshund 4986
196mm (7¾") *Long*

Beagle 5049
215mm (8½") *Long*

Boxer 5032
195mm (7¾") *Long*

Spaniel 5076
198mm (7¾") *Long*

Yorkshire Terrier 5027
138mm (5½") *High*

West Highland Terrier 4988
157mm (6¼") *Long*

▲ Hand decorated Supreme Dogs. Page from SylvaC catalogue c.1980.

Corgi 3128
108mm (4¼") *High*

Cairn Terrier 3447
127mm (5") *High*

Chow 3173
120mm (4¾") *High*

St. Bernard 2493
114mm (4½") *High*

Old English Sheep Dog 2675
127mm (5") *High*

Boston Terrier
114mm (4½") *High*

Spaniel 18
*(available in either Black & White
or Brown & White)*
127mm (5") *High*

Golden Labrador 3500
127mm (5") *High*

Jack Russell Terrier 3913
95mm (3½") *High*

▲ Hand decorated Dogs. Page from SylvaC catalogue c.1980.

King Charles Spaniel 4097
122mm (4¾") *High*

Greyhound 2537
191mm (7½") *Long*

Golden Retriever 3169
133mm (5¼") *High*

Poodle 2962
133mm (5¼") *High*

Pekingese 3165
76mm (3") *High*

Mongrel Puppy 2974
140mm (5½") *High*

Staffordshire Bull Terrier 3166
114mm (4½") *High*

Pug 3552
114mm (4½") *High*

Black Labrador 3500
127mm (5") *High*

▲ Hand decorated Dogs. Page from SylvaC catalogue c.1980.

Afghan Hound 5108
222mm (8¾") *Long*

Alsation 5112
248mm (9¾") *Long*

Dobermann Pinscher 5150
215mm (8½") *Long*

Shetland Sheepdog 5023
160mm (6¼") *High*

Golden Labrador 5167
240mm (9½") *Long*

Irish (Red) Setter 5170
235mm (9¼") *Long*

Welsh Sheep Dog 5205
250mm (9¾") *Long*

▲ Hand decorated Supreme Dogs. Page from SylvaC catalogue c.1980.

St. Bernard 5320
240 (9½") *Long*

Black Labrador 5167
240mm (9½") *Long*

Bassett Hound 3642
127mm (5") *Long*

Bulldog 16
133mm (5¼") *Long*

Bassett Hound 3561
146mm (5¾") *Long*

Dalmation 5034
228mm (9") *Long*

Collie 5000
228mm (9") *Long*

▲ Hand decorated Supreme Dogs. Page from SylvaC catalogue c.1980.

◀ Dog number 1203 9″ high. From the collection of and photograph by John Howard.

▲ Each dog is numbered 166, but the left hand dog is also marked No. 1. Although 166 is a Falcon number the dogs are marked SylvaC. Photograph by Peter Lepino.

*Dog 2938
102mm (4") *High*

*Dog 2950
133mm (5¼") *High*

•Dog 2951
178mm (7") *High*

Set of three sheepdogs, from left number 5303 3¼" high, ▶
5302 5¼" high and 5301 7" high.

*Dog 5297
95mm (3¾") *High*

•Dog 5295
178mm (7") *High*

*Dog 5296
133mm (5¼") *High*

*Dog 5293
140mm (5½") *High*

*Dog 5294
98mm (3⅞") *High*

•Dog 5292
180mm (7⅛") *High*

OTHER ANIMALS

Several new animals have been discovered since my last book, and these include two lions, numbers **818** and **819**. Numbers **822** and **825** are plinths on which the lions can sometimes be found standing. Lion number **819** on plinth number **825** has a container attached to it, which could have been used as a spill vase. It is possible the lions stood in the hearth or alongside the fireplace, the examples found have been black cellulose and look rather grand. Also sighted has been a camel number **772**, standing, with a howdah approximately 7″ high and 9″ long.

Although not a new number I have been sent a photograph of swan **795** by a collector, it is a wonderful piece in a cellulose finish and very nicely coloured. These swans were possibly used as part of a display in Dairy Shop windows, one elderly gentleman is sure he remembers seeing them filled with eggs. This is quite feasible as other Shaw & Copestake, SylvaC or Falcon Ware products have been used for this purpose.

Several cats have been located, number **843** is a black laughing cat about 8″h, it is sitting, has a white wing colour and red bow tie on a very long neck. An interesting fact about this cat is that it was given to Mrs. Violet Brown by Mr. William Shaw, the founder of Shaw & Copestake, in 1933, on the occasion of her wedding. Of course colours may vary on other examples found.

Cat number **1286** has been a recent find in blue, he is 4″h and there is speculation as to whether he has some larger companions. He sits with a surprised expression on his face, eyes wide open and mouth in shape of an O. He has a bow around his neck, and is pictured in the 1930s catalogue.

Cats, numbers **1159** 6¼″h, **1162** 3¾″h, **1163** 7¼″h and **1164** 11″h, have amazing corkscrew tails. This is one set on which I had no information and several different collectors now have various sizes. The cats are leaning on their elbows with tails in the air. As is the case with many SylvaC pieces they are quite extraordinary, so far they have been seen in dark brown, fawn and green all in a matt glaze.

An advert in the 1936 Pottery Gazette showed a family of ducks very smartly dressed, as if on their way to church. I had no idea of the numbers of the models, but have since found that Mrs. Duck is number **1157** 8″h and Mr. Duck is number **1158** 9″h. Both pieces are in a matt glaze but they were originally handpainted as well. Mrs. Duck is smartly dressed in a bonnet and shawl and clutching a purse, she even has a necklace, and is very much in the mould of Jemima Puddleduck. Mr. Duck is equally as smart, with a top hat, jacket and waistcoat, tie and wing collar. You can see from the original advert which has been reproduced from The Pottery Gazette, that all four boy ducks are the same, they have school caps, smart jackets and little bow ties, I have not been able to ascertain the mould number of Master Duck.

Penguin number **1290** shown in the 1930s catalogue has yet to be seen by a collector, so no further information regarding this. Hen ashtray and match holder number **1292** is a companion to the duck ashtray number **1293** and follows the style of animal ashtrays.

My mother suddenly realised a few months ago that the two rabbit ashtrays which had stood in our hearth during the 1940s were in fact SylvaC, they had been tucked away in a cupboard and forgotten for years, to re-emerge in triumph, the number is **1294** and can be seen in the 1930s catalogue. She can actually remember buying them at a store in Richmond-on-Thames in about 1941, for 1/6d. the pair. I'm sure homes all over the country have countless pieces of SylvaC tucked away in corners, that are forgotten for the moment.

Another interesting item seen in a 1930s catalogue is a rabbit tablemat holder, number **1255**, from the illustration this looks like half a rabbit of the round **1065** variety, split between the ears, on a base, it was originally supplied with the mats. I describe it as seen in the brochure, and have no idea of exact size. Has anyone information about this unique SylvaC item?

Dumbo the elephant is number **3140**, he certainly looks like the Walt Disney cartoon character, having very large ears. Although he is quite small he has bags of character, and has been nicely hand painted in fawn. Another elephant recently found has been number **3239**, it is exactly the same design as the old elephants numbers **814** and **815**, but is carrying china flowers on its back instead of a howdah, this particular one is a pretty shade of yellow. There is actually a space in the back of the elephant to accommodate the flowers.

Number **3927**, the fox feeding the chicken, with an axe behind his back was also based on a cartoon character according to his modeller George Matthews, and an expert on cartoons tells me it was probably the wily fox called Road Runner. It is mostly seen in a fawn matt colour but was also produced in hand painted natural colours. Also in this series is a smaller version of the fox, on tray number **4546** containing three chicken egg cups which have the same number. This is really delightful and represents all that SylvaC stands for, fine modelling with a tongue in cheek sense of humour.

Tortoise number **1464** in a collectors possession is most unusual, it is 3¼″ long and 2½″ high, in green matt and I would think was only produced for a very short time. It is like tortoise number 136 which has a shell lid and is a container, but **1464** is in one piece. Unfortunately the only example I have seen was badly damaged, the front legs had been broken, but at least it has survived for us to put in our records.

I can now confirm there is a set of three ski-ing ducks. The smallest **1678** 2″h, middle size **1679** 2¼″h and largest **1680** 5¼″h, they are all leaning in slightly different directions as can be seen in the photograph taken from a catalogue. These are generally found in the colour combination of green skis and fawn ducks, but no doubt someone will have them in a totally different colour!

▲ Lion number 818, from the collection of Darrell Willis-Utting.

▲ Tortoise number 1464 from the collection of Mrs. Jane Hallsworth. Photograph by Peter Lepino.

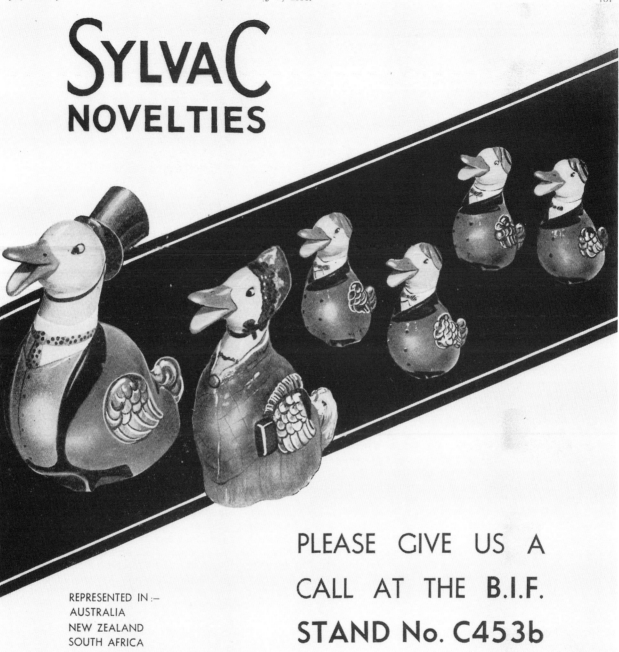

SYLVAC
NOVELTIES

REPRESENTED IN :—
AUSTRALIA
NEW ZEALAND
SOUTH AFRICA
CANADA
NORWAY
Etc.

PLEASE GIVE US A
CALL AT THE **B.I.F.**
STAND No. **C453b**

SHAW & COPESTAKE
SYLVAN WORKS, LONGTON

Telephone : Longton 3564.

LONDON AGENT : J. E. HOLT,
60, SHOE LANE, HOLBORN, E.C.4.
Telephone : Holborn 2447.

IRISH AGENT : H. DEAN,
41, DONEGALL PLACE, BELFAST.
Telephone : 2122.

▲ Advert in The Pottery Gazette 1st February 1936. Mrs.
Duck number 1157 8" high, Mr. Duck 1158 9" high.

▲ Page from a SylvaC catalogue c.1936/1937.

◀ Laughing cat number 843 8½″ high given to Mrs. Violet Brown by Mr. William Shaw. Photograph by Peter Lepino.

| *Cat 5299 | •Cat 5298 | *Cat 5300 |
| 133mm (5¼″) *High* | 180 (7⅛″) *High* | 98mm (3⅞″) *High* |

■ Rabbit ...	...	1386	...	3¼″ high
■ Rabbit ...	...	1067	...	4″ ,,
■ Rabbit ...	...	990	...	5″ ,,
● Rabbit ...	...	1026	...	6¾″ ,,
Rabbit ...	...	1028	...	10″ ,,
■ Rabbit ...	...	1509	...	4″ ,,
■ Rabbit ...	...	1302	...	5¼″ ,,
■ Hare ...	...	1298	...	5¾″ ,,
■ Cat ...	...	1046	...	6″ ,,
Cat ...	...	3392	...	12¾″ ,,

■ *Items marked thus sold in minimum quantities of* 12

● *Items marked thus sold in minimum quantities of* 6

▲ Page from an original SylvaC catalogue.

◀ Elephant in football gear, number 1238 8″ high. Photograph by Peter Lepino.

◀ 'Dumbo' the elephant number 3140 5″ long. From the collection of Darrell Willis-Utting.

Elephant with hand painted flowers, number 3239. From ▶ the collection of and photograph by Mrs. Jane Hallsworth.

SYLVAC

1678 2"

1679 2¾"

1680 5¼"

1498 3½"

1499 4½"

1492 6"

PIXIE 1420 3¼"

BEAR 134 5½"

1390 4½"

FOX 1424

▲ Page from a SylvaC catalogue c.1950.

◀ ▼ Page from a SylvaC catalogue.

THE
NOBLEST
ANIMAL OF THEM ALL

3180 WHITE

HORSE 3180 - 9″ high

The 'Shire' by *SylvaC*

Shire Horse 4872 (either in Brown or Grey decoration)
330 mm (13″) long, 245 mm (9¾″) high
(Also available without harness)

◀ Rare Swan number 795. From
the collection of and photograph
by Stuart Sherwood.

FIGURES

It was a very exciting day for me when a collector sent a wonderful photograph of a Red Indian Chief, sitting on a grass mound, colourfully decorated in a cellulose finish. The mould number is **1033** it is 7¼" high, and has an original silver 1930s style SylvaC label still on the base, (see page 68 The SylvaC Story). It looks in remarkable condition, and I should imagine is a highly prized SylvaC piece.

The Dancing Lady figures are part of the old Shaw & Copestake range. Three different dancers have so far been found, they are the Spanish lady number **881** 9½" high, a lady holding one side of her skirt number **919** 8½"h and a lady holding two sides of her skirt number **920** 8½"h. The colour combinations are usually black tops with red or orangey/yellow skirts, in the cellulose finish, they are sometimes found in blue or green matt glazes, the matt figures considered the most desirable by collectors. The condition of the figures seem to vary, if a favourite position for displaying it was on the window-sill the inevitable fading by sunlight occurs on the cellulose examples, but if it was tucked away in a china cabinet it can be found in pristine condition. They were probably only produced for a few years, prior to World War II, but are relatively easy to find, the prices vary between ten pounds and a hundred pounds depending on condition.

I also have a Pierrot in my own collection number **931** 8¾"h, coloured in red and black, and I have no doubt there is also a Pierrette to partner him somewhere. This figure is much more unusual, and I have only heard of one other collector with an example, in the traditional black and white Peirrot colours.

Fortunately all the Shaw & Copestake figures are very clearly numbered, they have the typical Shaw & Copestake 'Made in England' mark, and can be easily identified. The Pierrot also had a 1930s SylvaC silver printed label on it. The bases of the figures are all slightly different, depending on the style. I found one on a typical 1930s table lamp, quite a few SylvaC pieces have been used in this way.

When on a visit to the SylvaC factory in 1989 I also sighted a Madonna type figure and a Joan of Arc, unfortunately I do not have the numbers for these items. But they are worth looking out for.

Collectors may be interested in the four figures in the Country Craft range. They are Girl and Dog number 5313, Girl and Goat usually marked Alice on the base number 5314, Gamekeeper marked Adam on the base number 5315 and Goose Girl number 5316 all about 11½" high. These have so far been found in pinky/fawn and light blue glossy colours, they were also originally hand decorated in natural colours. Some of them have 'Staffordshire Rustics' on the base.

According to the modeller George Matthews, there is no special story behind these items, his brief was originally to design some typical Staffordshire pottery figures similar to the old flat back designs. Although these are not flat backs, they are of the same style. Girl and Goat (Alice) features a young girl with hat and ringlets, leaning against a rather depressed looking goat with two horns, she has a basket of fruit and flowers at her feet. Gamekeeper (Adam) is in breeches and waistcoat carries a shotgun and is accompanied by his dog. He leans against a tree, a rabbit can be seen peeping around the trunk.

The two models I have seen have plenty of detail in them, but are certainly an acquired taste, like many SylvaC pieces they probably grow on you gradually. I am sure they look much nicer in the hand painted natural colours, and I look forward to seeing an example one day.

▲ Adam the Gamekeeper number 5315 and Alice with Goat number 5314.
From the collection of Malcolm Harris. Photograph by Glyn Steadman.

▲ A selection of typical old Shaw & Copestake black vases, from the left vase number 425 9″ high 'Moonlight Ware' decoration number 1500, vase number 419 11½″ high, rose bowl number 575 8½″ high with decoration number 1760, vase number 273 9″ high 'Venetian' (registered number 716616 for the decoration), decoration number 1977, vase number 421 7½″ high decoration number 1907. All these vases have the old Shaw & Copestake 'Daisy' mark.

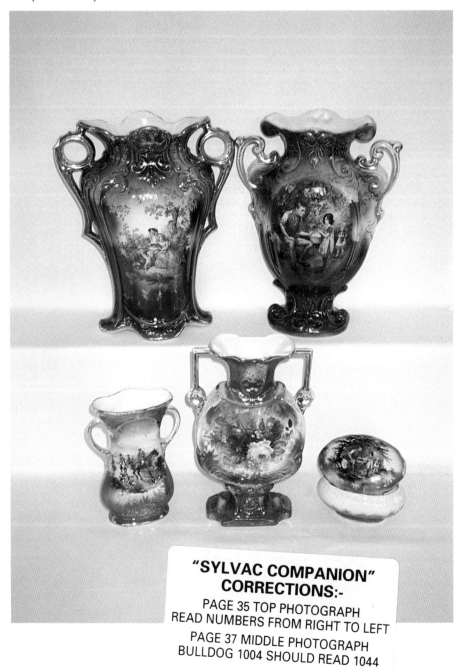

◀ A selection of typical old Shaw & Copestake brown vases, top left number 374 11¼″ high, right number 337 12″ high, left number 578 6¼″ high, centre number 600 9¼″ high. Trinket box 4¾″ long is unmarked except for a printed 'Made in England' which exactly matches one on vase number 337, it also has the same decoration.

▼ An extraordinary corkscrew tailed cat, number 1163 7¼″ high, registered number 806569 (1935/1936). From the collection of Darrell Willis-Utting. Photograph by Nigel Willis-Utting.

"SYLVAC COMPANION"
CORRECTIONS:-
PAGE 35 TOP PHOTOGRAPH
READ NUMBERS FROM RIGHT TO LEFT
PAGE 37 MIDDLE PHOTOGRAPH
BULLDOG 1004 SHOULD READ 1044

▲ Some of the old Shaw & Copestake figures, in a cellulose finish. From the left number 920 8½" high. Pierrot number 931 8¾" high, Spanish dancer number 881 9½" high, figure number 919 8½" high. They can also be found in matt colours.

◄ The amazing Red Indian Chief number 1033 7¼" high, found by Mrs. Hazel Cossey. It has an original SylvaC label on the base. Photograph by Robert Cossey.

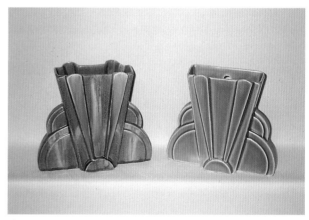

▲ On the left Art Deco style vase number 1109, and matching wall vase number 1384.

Old Shaw & Copestake plant pot number 127 showing two different decorations. From the collection of Malcolm Harris, photograph by Glyn Steadman.   ▼

▲ A lovely old Shaw & Copestake clock number 604 12″ high decoration number 2216. From the collection of Darrell Willis-Utting.

▲ From the left vase number 839 registered number 774557 (1932/1933) with the very popular Egyptian design. Poppy ginger jar number 903 and a Wild Duck vase number 784. They can also be found in matt colours. From the collection of David Richards.

Some early Shaw & Copestake dogs, from the left dog number 1117, dog number 743 attached to vase number 827 and bulldog number 1004. All in a cellulose finish. ▶

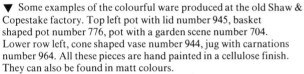

▼ Some examples of the colourful ware produced at the old Shaw & Copestake factory. Top left pot with lid number 945, basket shaped pot number 776, pot with a garden scene number 704. Lower row left, cone shaped vase number 944, jug with carnations number 964. All these pieces are hand painted in a cellulose finish. They can also be found in matt colours.

An old Shaw & Copestake jug and bowl marked Silvo, with a very striking decoration. The bowl is 15″ diameter and the jug 11″ high. Photograph by Peter Lepino. ▼

▲ A selection of jugs number 573 in varying sizes, they can be found with many different decorations. Top right is jug number 560 which is hexagonal. From the collection of Malcolm Harris, photograph by Glyn Steadman.

A wonderful selection of Falcon Ware from the collection of Malcolm Harris. The clockset vases are marked ESSEX, and inside the base of the clock is inscribed 'To Minnie from Lily and Florrie Xmas 1931'. Photograph by Glyn Steadman. ▼

▲ Benjamin was my constant companion whilst compiling the information for this book. He sits with his friend 'Big' Mac, number 1209 11″ high.

These Joey dogs have been brought together with the help of Darrell Willis-Utting, who is the proud owner of the fawn and green examples. From the left, number 1191, number 1192, number 1193 and number 1194. ▼

▲ A SylvaC dog 5¼″ high, holding a pipe in its mouth, the number is indecipherable. Photograph by Peter Lepino.

From left, small dog number 1120 3¾″ high, dog number 2331 5¼″ high, dog with one paw raised number 1475 7¼″ high, all from the collection of Darrell Willis-Utting, and dog with slipper number 3827 5″ high. ▼

◄ Two puppy companions, number 1646 is playing and number 1647, belonging to Darrell Willis-Utting, is sleeping.

The Bonnie Galloway ashtray, number 4972 was specially commissioned for the Galloway Bull Society, possibly only about 200 were originally made. The 'Le Moulin de Lecq Inn' ashtray was also specially made for a well-known Jersey nightspot of that name, it has no number. The 'With compliments of SylvaC' ashtray/posy, number 2970 4½″ long, were given away to customers and clients of the Shaw & Copestake factory. ▼

▲ Jenny Hulme with her amazing collection of SylvaC rabbits. Jenny is holding the blue rabbit which was her very first SylvaC piece. Photograph by Jenny Hulme.

A 'Crinoline Lady' sandwich set from the collection of Jayne L'Epine-Smith, jug decorated with 'Down Somerset Way', powder bowl with 'Glorious Devon', vase marked 'Victor' on base and decorated with 'The old Mill', jug with decoration number 4706. All Falcon Ware. ▼

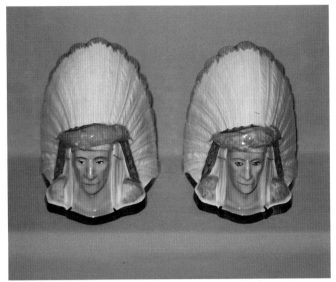

▲ Colourful Red Indian Chief bookends, they have the decoration number 4961 and are marked Falcon Ware.

▲ This Falcon Ware Hound tankard has no number. Notice how cleverly the dogs lead forms the handle. Photograph by Peter Lepino.

◀ A Falcon Ware tray and set of jugs from the collection of and photograph by Jenny Hulme.

▼ Ideal SylvaC ornaments for the Nursery, standing Mule number 3384. Sitting Mule number 3383 kindly loaned by Darrell Willis-Utting.

▼ SylvaC Galloway Bull number 5207 8″ long 5½″ high. Photograph by Peter Lepino.

▲ A Falcon Ware jug and bowl with a lovely Willow Pattern. The decoration number is 4435. From the collection of Malcolm Harris, photograph by Glyn Steadman.

◀ A wonderful display of Shaw & Copestake flower jugs and vases, from the collection of Malcom Harris. Note the unusual blue embossed hollyhock vase centre of back row number 1114, and also the Egyptian design jug number 829 on the right of front row. Photograph by Glyn Steadman.

▼ Old Shaw & Copestake vases. The toothbrush holder has no number or mark, the centre vase is number 614 9¾″ high, the vase on the right is part of a clockset and numbered 606 it also has a gold 'Daisy' and 'Moonlight Ware'. The two smaller vases are number 780, and the decoration is called 'Old English Inns'.

▼ This wonderful Falcon Ware Toucan 9½″ high, is from the collection of Darrell Willis-Utting. On the base is: Toucan - Falcon ware, -Grecian. Grecian being the colour description. Photograph by Nigel Willis-Utting.

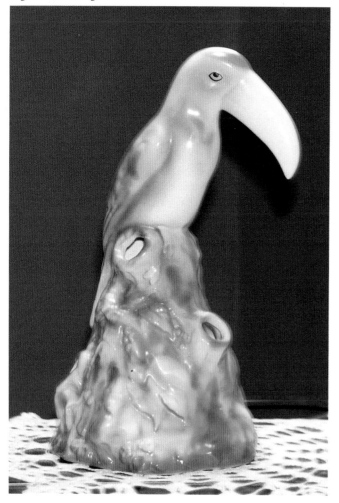

▼ Falcon Ware biscuit barrel marked Haddon decoration number 5146, bread plate decoration number 4912 'Glorious Devon', and jug decorated with 'A bit of Old England'.

TABLEWARE

Although tableware was produced in the early days at the Shaw & Copestake factory I am going to concentrate on some of the SylvaC tableware produced from the 1930s.

I have reproduced one of the pages from a 1930s catalogue showing some of the range available at that time. The ware is of a vertical ribbed design, and consists of a set of six mugs **1090** with a cider jug **1091**, cruet and stand **1183**, honey pot **1184**, butter dish **1213**, biscuit jar 1216, posy rings 1248 and 1250, and a rather unusual rabbit table mat stand **1255**. This range was available in matt colours of blue, green, brown, ivory, fawn and grey, and could also be suppled in 'pleasing applied decorations'. I have some of this range in my collection, it has a nice homely feel to it, and was probably very popular in its time.

Similar wares but with a slanting incised design were produced about the same time, the numbers are sifter 1362, jug **1363**, mug **1364**, jam pot 1365, and butter dish 1368. The jugs and mugs were usually described as lemonade sets. It is mostly seen in green matt or blue matt both very rich colours, and can be found in good condition, it was a solid serviceable everyday set.

A barrel design followed a year or two later, this had a wood grain effect with, on the larger pieces, two horizontal lines to represent the metal bands around a barrel. It was similar to the ribbed design and consisted of a jug 1435, mug **1436**, honey/jam pot 1437, butter or cheese dish **1438**, cruet 1439, small butter or sweet dish 1440, cigarette barrel 1441, match barrel 1442, sauce bottle holder or vase 1443, mint sauce boat 1445, biscuit jar 1446, and serviette ring 1459. This was available in a matt glaze of green, fawn, blue, pink and ivory, the serviette ring had the smallest hare attached and probably this was produced independently in a larger range of colours.

During World War II, the Dahlia range of tableware was introduced, this had an embossed Dahlia pattern on each piece, and was available in matt colours of green, blue, fawn, cream and white. Some pieces can also be found in glossy pastel colours of blue and pink. There was a cruet 1572, mug 1579, jugs in three sizes 1580, honey pot 1581, butter dish 1582, sugar bowl 1583, cream jug 1584, teapot 1585, cheese dish 1586, biscuit jar 1587 had a cane handle.

All these tableware ranges have the most delightful cruet sets on stands, which are very collectable, but a word of warning. I have bought several only to find them disintegrate before my eyes when I wash them, as the salt seems to eat into the pottery. The salt has probably been left in the cruet for years, and become damp, and then dried out to have this effect. It will pay you to inspect the cruets carefully for signs of this before purchase.

NEPTUNE ware, only recently discovered, thanks to a collector, was first produced in the 1940s. It consisted of cheese dish **1747**, large tray **1748**, small tray **1797**, twin tray **1798**, these pieces have a pale blue body and white handles, (Wedgwood colours). NEPTUNE was made with a blue clay body, and not using a blue glaze, this blue clay body was only used in the Thomas Lawrence (Falcon Ware) factory, and not at the Shaw & Copestake factory. There was also a teapot 1812, sugar bowl with two handles 1813, cream jug **1814** and a set of jugs **1815** in three sizes, all in a blue colour with an incised pattern of waves and a seahorse on each piece. Although having Shaw & Copestake numbers they were made in the Falcon Ware factory and most have the Falcon mark on the base. I have only seen one piece, the tray 1748, which I have in my collection.

Also produced around the same time as NEPTUNE was SPRINGBOK, possibly originally for the South African market as at this time only seconds of decorated wares were allowed to be sold on the home market. A comparatively small quantity was produced. Springbok meaning – *gazelle with habit of springing in play or when alarmed* – is the national emblem of South Africa. Each piece is beautifully decorated with a Springbok leaping

between two large leaves, hand painted in green and orange on a white satin matt glaze. The range consists of a teapot which carries no number, tray F**262**, honey pot F**266**, cream jug F**267**, covered sugar bowl F**268**, vases F**275** and F**276**, bowl F**277**. The teapot, cream jug and honeypot have flat circular sides to them so typical of the 1930s and 1940s. (See photograph reproduced from the catalogue). They have the low Falcon Ware numbers, and as they were only made in the Thomas Lawrence factory are probably marked Falcon Ware.

ENGLISH ROSE tableware was made in the 1940s at the Falcon Ware factory. For some reason ENGLISH ROSE carries no numbers, it was available in pastel shades of pink and primrose, the handles were leaf green. It consisted of a teaset, cheese dish, honey pot, three sizes of lemonade jugs, three sizes of salad bowls, sandwich tray, sweet dish, fruit bowl and a mug. A little later a coffee set and toilet ware was added to the range. Many years later in 1977, it was re-introduced with numbers ranging from 5409 to 5418, so numbered pieces are the later range, which was also made in pastel colours.

What an unusual tableware set the DOGS HEAD range is. Each piece has a little dogs head peaping out as if from a box. The cruet number 1715, consists of a tray with two handles and three cruets, the little mustard pot is the only piece which has a different dogs head, all the other pieces have the dog with either the right or left ear up, but the mustard pot dog has both ears down. Part of this range, without the dog heads are jug **1728** and sugar bowl **1765**. The rest of the range is a butter dish 1818, jam pot 1849, cheese dish 1850 and a toast rack 1990. The general design is of a wooden box with horizontal bands round where appropriate. The colours are usually green with a fawn dog, but can be found fawn with a green dog. It was produced from the late 1940s until the 1960s.

Another new design after World War II, first introduced in 1949, was BLACKBERRY, described as '*A pattern with a delicately mottled body, supplied in either Rose Pink or Primrose with simple hand-painted blackberry motifs in relief*'. There was a tea set, a coffee set, and various sized jugs, trays and hors d'oeuvre dishes, between the numbers of 1862 and **1876**. Some pieces such as a small square shallow dish, carry no numbers. New numbers in this range keep cropping up and it seems quite extensive, my dream is that one day I will find a complete teaset. I have not yet found any of the coffee set, but otherwise have a few pieces of BLACKBERRY. It is seen fairly frequently, and sometimes is very badly marked with black stains. I think some of the jugs and dishes were actually used for blackberries or a blackcurrant drink which is well known for its staining properties. I have so far found no way of eradicating these marks.

NULEEF as the name suggests, has an embossed leaf pattern on each piece. It was available in pastel matt shades of stone, yellow, turquoise and orange. The numbers are scattered between **2333** and **2367** and it was produced during the 1950s and 1960s. As far as I know there was no teapot or cups and saucers, but every other piece of tableware was included, also a wall vase, bulb bowl, vases and posy trough. I have a few of these pieces in different colours, they are nicely made and inexpensive to buy at the moment as the design is not very exciting. I find it challenging to try and make up complete sets of tableware.

WYKA tableware has a wicker basket effect, and was available in amber, green matt, and yellow matt. The colours are quite vibrant making this fun to collect. There is no record of a teaset being available in WYKA although a full set of tableware was offered, the numbers are spread between 2956 and 3013, a beaker, number 3012 was included. This was produced during the 1960s and although pieces are often found these days, does not seem to have been continued for very long.

The first pieces of the ubiquitous AVON ware were produced in the late 1960s starting with beaker 2945. Different pieces of tableware were added over the years, and it consisted of eighteen or twenty-one piece teasets, an early morning set, a fruit set and fifteen piece coffee set. With every conceivable type of tableware available to compliment the sets. Although the AVON tableware was a plain shape with no embellishments at all, decorations were added by way of transfers, or lithographs. By far the most popular decoration was Limegrove, which was a pattern of blue leaves and blue flowers on a white matt background. This decoration is also widely used by other manufacturers and can be seen on other teasets and tableware, not made by SylvaC.

The other AVON ware decorations are Nicole which has pink flowers, on a white matt background, and Summer Reverie, which has a blue and orange flower on a beige background. A few of the pieces do not carry numbers, notably the jollied wares, which are not made from a mould and are mainly plates and bowls. The numbers are scattered between 2945 and 3636. The flat cheese board and knife number 3297, is an interesting piece as I understand it is very difficult to make a flat piece of pottery due to the possibility of cracking or distortion, and this was considered quite an achievement. There is also a charming cheese and biscuit tray number 3636.

Very rarely seen is BUTTERFLY ware, modelled in 1964 by Reginald Thompson, the numbers are scattered between 3554 and 3746. I don't have many of these pieces in my collection yet, but live in hopes of gradually building up a set. At the moment I have honey pot number 3576, pale yellow and white with a butterfly handle, the cruet set number 3619, with a butterfly on the tray and mustard pot, in pale green and white, sandwich tray number **3745**, white with a butterfly motif at one corner, and two white cups which carry no number, with butterfly handles. No doubt they were also produced in colours other than those mentioned, but please note that I can only describe pieces I have seen, which doesn't rule out other colour combinations. To my knowledge, there appears to be no advertising material or reference in the catalogues to this range.

MEDWAY is best described as a pebbledash finish, it has a similarly rough surface. In the Mould Makers register the word 'grit' appears after each mention, so perhaps grit is actually added to the slip to achieve this effect. I may sound very odd, but is in fact quite dramatic. It was available in only two colours, cottage red and studio green, a tea set, dinner set and various oddments were available as well as about eight different styles of vases. It definitely has the rustic look, and is certainly 'different', it was produced during the 1970s and the numbers are between 4797 and 4882.

Tableware for special occasions also featured at the SylvaC factory and HOLLYBERRY for the Christmas table probably tops the list. Each piece was either holly shaped or carried the holly design, it was dark green with hand painted red berries. It consisted of candlestick 4396, trays 4398 and 4399, honey 4530, cheese dish 4576, cruet 4577, posy 4579, posy ring 4580, candlestick 4582 (to fit posy 4580), vase 4629, beaker 4633, tray 4634 and jardiniere 4646. This was quite adequate for decorating the Christmas table without overdoing the effect. It was produced during the 1960s and 1970s, there is no record as to who modelled it.

ANNIVERSARY was decorated with roses, wedding bells, bows and hearts. It was available in blue/white, gold/pale green, silver/pale pink, and included honey 5447, goblet 5448, teapot 5449, plate 5450, powder bowl **5451**, cream 5452, cup 5453, saucer 5454, tea plate 5455, loving cup 5456, bowl 5457, tray 5458, candlestick 5459, bell 5460. It was produced during the years 1978–1981. Sixteen numbers were originally reserved for this range but only fourteen actually used, and was modelled by George Matthews. The heart shaped powder bowl was pressed into service, suitably decorated in a regal manner, to celebrate the wedding of the Prince and Princess of Wales in 1981.

Next we come to the baby ranges, there were two decorations one called ZOOLINE NURSERY WARE, and the other TEDDY NURSERY RANGE. The same shapes were used for both, and the numbers are plate 3262, plate 3263, cereal dish 3264, beaker with two handles 3617, beaker with one handle 3742, egg cup **3788**, and baby plate 3791. With ZOOLINE came a later addition of an engine 5479 with two egg cup trucks number 5478, produced in 1981. ZOOLINE was colourfully decorated with a steam engine carrying animal passengers in an open carriage, on a cream background. ZOOLINE baby plate number 3791, which I have in my collection, is the only piece I have every seen that has a mark on the base which states it was made by Shaw & Copestake. This seems to be quite a rarity as at no time during their 82 years of manufacturing do they seem to use their name on the ware.

I also have in my collection egg cup number **3788** beautifully hand decorated with pastel flowers, in the style of Radford. On the base it has 'hand painted by E.F. Nelson', no one seems to have heard of this person, so perhaps it was one of the plain pieces passed on to another pottery for decoration. The TEDDY NURSERY RANGE is also very colourful and has various Teddy characters following different pursuits, and a band of Teddy Bears around the edges rather in the style of the Doulton Bunnykins range. There does not seem to be any hand painting on these pieces, but this doesn't detract from the overall effect of colour required for childrens ware. Most of the nursery ware items were produced from the 1960s and production continued until 1989 even after the take-over of the Sylvan works by Crown Winsor.

In the late 1940s or early 1950s, Falcon Ware produced a small set of PLAYTIME Nursery pieces. There is an advert for the set in the Pottery Gazette and Glass Trade Review dated August 1952. It is possible this set was actually produced before that date, but I can find no record of it, and none of the pieces have a mould number to help with the dating. There seem to be only three pieces, a beaker with one handle, a cereal bowl and a baby plate, but it is likely other pieces such as plates were also decorated. The decoration is of Koala Bears playing cricket, with a band of Kangaroos around the edge of the wares. The connection with Australia immediately comes to mind, and these could have been specially made for that market. Possibly the pieces were also marked SylvaC, but they were certainly made at the Falcon Works.

I cannot conclude this chapter on tableware without mentioning TOTEM range, which was modelled by Mr. George Matthews. This has a very shiny finish and was available in colours described as Aventurine, Golden Peat, Peat Green and Trans Blue. It was very extensive and included a breakfast set, tea and dinner set, kitchen ware, coffee maker set which included packets of filter paper and an instruction book. It was produced in the 1960s and 1970s and has an incised design of circles round the edge with different shaped lines between the circles. It seems to have a particularly shiny finish which makes it look fresh and clean. The numbers are scattered between 3977 and 4357 and frequently seen, it should be relatively easy to make up a complete set.

▲ Page from a SylvaC catalogue c.1936/1937.

▼ Page from a SylvaC catalogue c.1942, showing Dahlia tableware.

1587	1580	1579	1585	1586	1572
Biscuit Jar	Jugs (Made in 3 Sizes)	Mug	Teapot	Cheese Dish	Cruet

1591	1583	1584	1581	1582	1589
Butter	Sugar	Cream	Honey	Butter	Butter, 4″ diameter

▲ Page from a Falcon catalogue c. 1949.

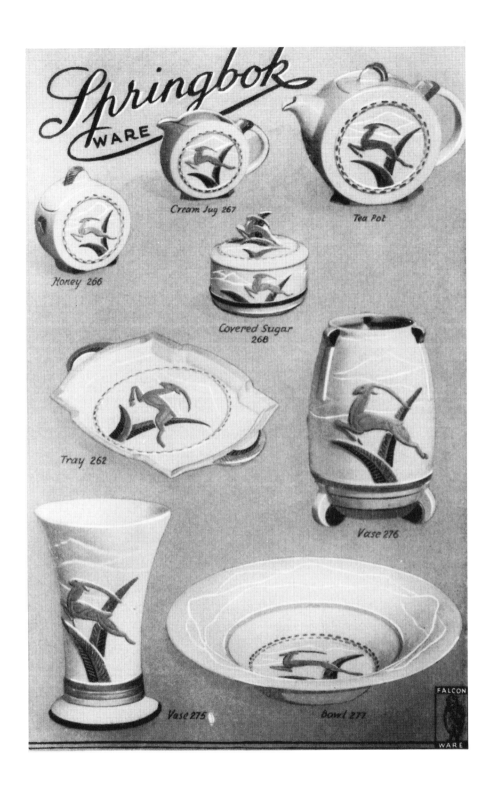

▲ Page from a Falcon catalogue c.1949.

▲ Nuleef range.

▲ Nuleef range.

2616   2611   2614   2619   2617

2636   2613   2638

2602   2615   2568   2610   2634

2612   2621   2608

▲ Laronde range.

Hodnet

Countryside

Indian Tree

Monaco

◀ Severn range, showing decorations available. Jug 5429
4½″ high, teapot 5419 5½″ high, cheese dish 5402 8¼″ long.
Cruet two piece 5400 3½″ high.

49

▲▼ Avon Shape. Limegrove pattern.

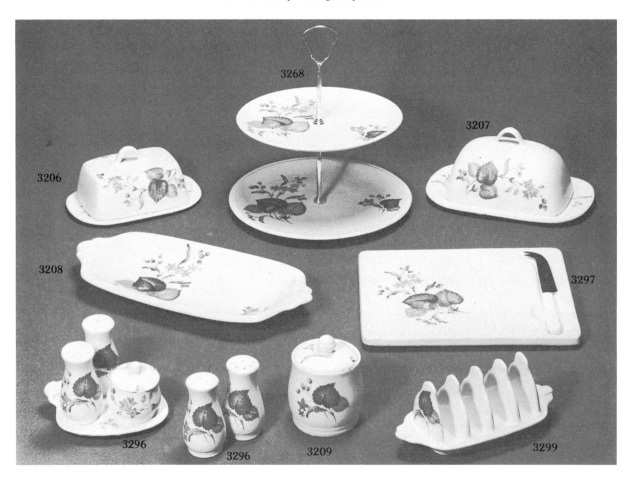

CUP 4851 & SAUCER 4850

4807

4852

4853

▲ Brazil range. (Dark brown with green leaf.)

4878

4806

4801

4882

4797

CUP 4843

4874

SAUCER 4844

4881

4876

4875

4880

4802

4877

4879

▲ Medway range tableware.

5450

5448

5449

5452

5451

5447

5459

5456

5460

5458

▲ Anniversary range.

"HOLLYBERRY" RANGE

Red Painting on Green Ground

approx. sizes

Vase	..	..	..	4629	.. ..	152mm (6″) high
Posy	..	..	..	4579	.. ..	170mm (6¾″) long
Posy (ring)	..	..	4580	.. ..	178mm (7″) across
Jardiniere	..	..	4646	.. ..	190mm (7½″) long
Tray	..	..	..	4399	.. ..	152mm (6″) ,,
Tray	..	..	..	4398	.. ..	203mm (8″) ,,
Tray	..	..	..	4634	.. ..	240mm (9½″) ,,
Candlestick	..	..	4396	.. ..	108mm (4¼″) across
Candlestick (to fit 4580)		4582	.. ..	76mm (3″) ,,
Beaker	..	..	..	4633	.. ..	90mm (3½″) high
Cruet	..	..	..	4577	.. ..	170mm (6¾″) long
Honey	..	..	..	4530	.. ..	102mm (4″) high
Cheese	..	..	..	4576	.. ..	184mm (7¼″) long

SHAW & COPESTAKE LTD, Sylvan Works, Longton, Stoke-on-Trent, ST3 1PW, England
Telephone: 33037/8 (STD 0782)

4014
4022
4029
4037
3982
4032
4033
4202
4039
4031
4036
4040
4038
3977
4030
3986

Totem range. ▲▼▶

4224
4140

CUP AND
SAUCER

10" PLATE OR
BREAD AND
BUTTER

8" PLATE

6½" PLATE

3977

▲ SylvaC coffee beakers.

▼ Cordon Brun range.

Colour selection: **Green—Pink—Primrose—White**

Tea Plate 5413
171mm (6¾") *across*

Tea Pot 5409 (4/5 cup)
127mm (5") *high*

Sugar Bowl 5410
102mm (4") *across*

Cream Jug 5411
77mm (3") *high*

Cup 5414
76mm (3") *high*

Saucer 5412
141mm (5½") *across*

▲ English Rose range.

▼ Trays, colour selection: Chinese Blue, Marigold, 'Pewter', Spring Green.

4197

4244

4198

4196

4195

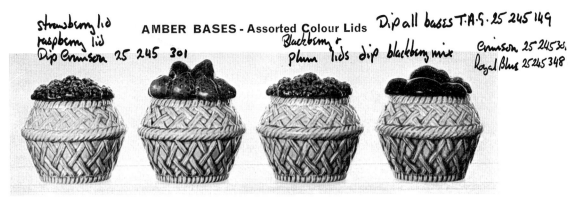

AMBER BASES - Assorted Colour Lids

Basket 'Honey' 4865
Bramble
95 mm (3¾") high

Basket 'Honey' 4865
Strawberry
100 mm (4") high

Basket 'Honey' 4865
Raspberry
95 mm (3¾") high

Basket 'Honey' 4865
Plum (Damson)
100 mm (4") high

Sold only in minimum quantities of 24 assorted

SylvaC

Household Novelties

All measurements are approximate

Beige Base — Assorted Colour Lids

Holder 4906
Pan Scourer
(Min. 3)
83 mm (3¼") high

Holder 4906
Beef Stock Cubes
(Min. 3)
83 mm (3¼") high

Holder 4906
Chicken Stock Cubes
(Min 3)
83 mm (3¼") high

All items on this page sold in minimum quantities (assorted colours) as stated

Green Bases — Assorted Colour Lids

Leaf 'Honey' 4871
Strawberry
95 mm (3¾") high

Leaf 'Honey' 4871
Bramble
90 mm (3½") high

Leaf 'Honey' 4871
Plum (Damson)
95 mm (3¾") high

Leaf 'Honey' 4871
Raspberry
90 mm (3½") high

Sold only in minimum quantities of 24 assorted

SHAW & COPESTAKE LTD., Sylvan Works, Longton, Stoke-on-Trent, ST3 1PN, England
Telephone: 33037/8 (STD 0782)

▲ Page from an original decorators catalogue.

"AGE OF CHIVALRY" TANKARDS

4245 (16 Fl. ozs – 4½" high approx.)

Litho and Gilt on white ground.
(Sold only in **sets of 6** as below)

| Edward Plantagenet The Black Prince | Sir Harry "Hotspur" Percy | Thomas Beauchamp Earl of Warwick | Ralph De Monthermer Earl of Gloucester and Hertford | John de Warenne Earl of Surrey and Sussex | Humphrey de Bohun Earl of Hereford and Essex |

▼▲ Pages from a SylvaC catalogue.

5284 'Castles'

5282 'Brass Rubbings'

5281 'King Arthur & Knights of the Round Table'

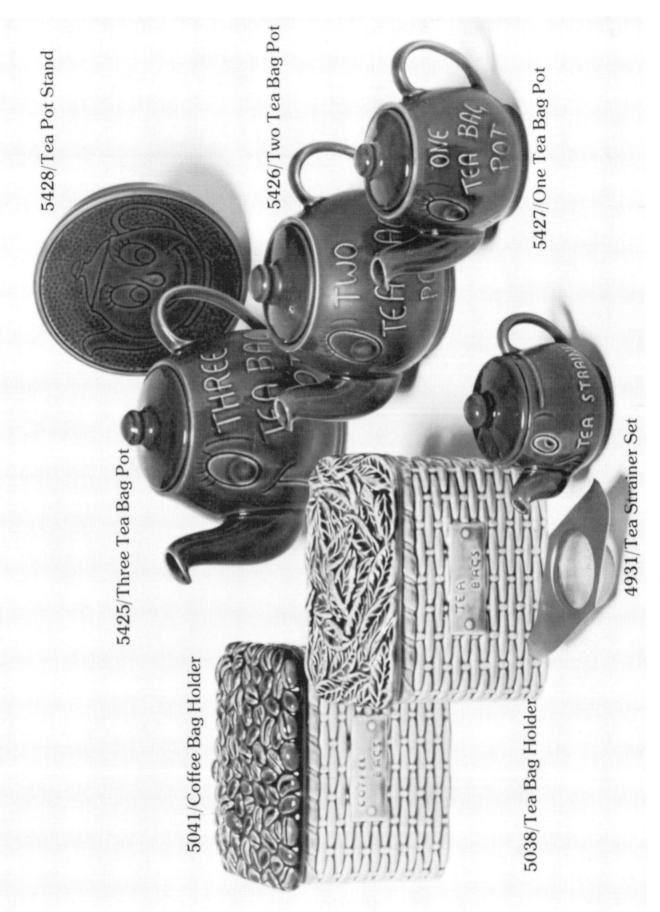

5428/Tea Pot Stand

5426/Two Tea Bag Pot

5427/One Tea Bag Pot

5425/Three Tea Bag Pot

4931/Tea Strainer Set

5041/Coffee Bag Holder

5038/Tea Bag Holder

▲ Household Novelties. From a SylvaC catalogue.

▲ Household Novelties. From a SylvaC catalogue.

5383

5466

5148

5272

5465

5043

5033

4683

5042

4317

4318

4267

4270

4255

4311

4253

4295

4254

4296

4275

4274

4273

▲ Pewter coloured glaze tankards.

61

4311
4273
4255
4270
4259
4218
4271
4318
4317

▲ Agincourt range.

▼ Pisces range.

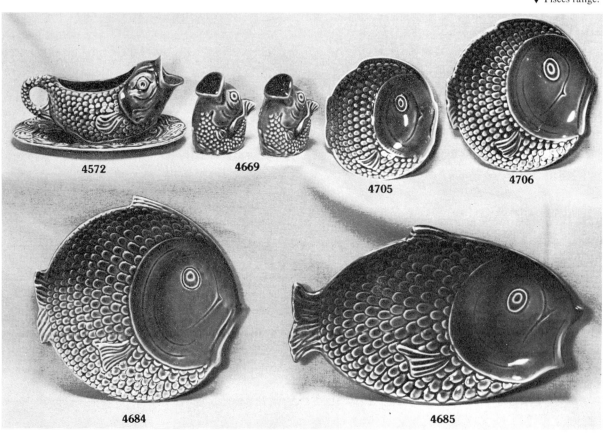

4572   **4669**   **4705**   **4706**

4684   **4685**

4574

4584

4570

2343

3278

2518

4719

2375

3274

3273

2376

2516

4125

2517

▲Tankards and ashtrays.

▼ Heather and Thistle range.

Covered Bowl **5272**
108mm (4¼") *across*

Honey or
Preserve Jar **3209**
100 mm (4") *high*

Vase **3040**
95mm (3¼") *high*

Beaker **2945**
108mm (4¼") *high*

Horseshoe Tray **5382**
152mm (6") *long*

Cream Jug **3204**
97mm (3¾") *high*

Sugar Bowl **2977**
82mm (3¼") *across*

63

VASE RANGES

This heading refers to some of the more interesting or unusual ranges produced by SylvaC or Falcon Ware. They consist of vases, flower pots, bulb pots, posy troughs, wall vases etc., and some tableware.

One of the first SYLVAC vase ranges was SHELL numbers **1272, 1275** to **1283**, introduced in the 1930s. It had vertical bands with horizontal loops within each band, giving a basket or wicker effect. It consisted of flower vases, flower jugs, flower holders, a fruit bowl and flower trough. It was supplied in matt glazes, a cellulose finish and art finishes. The art finish was described as follows:

'Executed in an entirely new and striking style of decoration, consisting of the blending of tones to resemble the colouring of shells:- 0343-having a green top blending down to a soft tone of yellow, pink rising from the foot. 0344-a pinkish-brown top blending down to yellow and having a bluey-green foot'.

The numbers 0343 and 0344 were the decoration numbers, and these descriptions show how the blending of the colours was first introduced during the mid 1930s, these decorations were available in a glazed or cellulose finish. The fruit bowl **1278**, flower pots 1282 and 1283 continued until 1970, but the other pieces were discontinued before 1939. Some new pieces of SHELL were introduced by the Falcon Factory in 1956 and were a very similar design, with the vertical and horizontal ribbed effect, but the base of the vases had a curved wave pattern, to represent the waves of the sea. The numbers of the later SHELL are F509 to F514. These were produced in white matt, and coloured pastel shades, as well as the blended colours. Much later, in the 1960s a NEW SHELL range was introduced, numbers 3523 to 3534 and 3562.

There was also a set of flower jugs, flower pots and vases in a horizontal ribbed pattern, amongst which are flower jugs **1070, 1150** vase **1173**, flower pots **1178, 1214, 1215**, and **1267** to **1269**. They were available in the following decoration numbers which I quote from the 1936/7 catalogue:

Cellulose Patterns in 'SylvaC' Ware

0323 – Floral daisy design, flowers in yellow and orange tints, backgrounds and other colourings in brown.

0353 – Crocus design in similar colourings to 0323.

0354 – Red floral design on ivory ground finish in brown and gold.

0355 – Floral border design in similar colourings to 0323.

0356 – Floral design in pleasing shades of pink, ground in mottled matt buff, finished in brown and gold.

It is interesting to note that an Australian collector sent a photograph of flower jug number **1150** in an 'art finish' of red and orange blending into blue and green which is quite stunning. These patterns were designed to match the modern furnishings and colour schemes of the time. Quite a few other flower pots, vases and flower jugs, flower troughs and flower holders, had a horizontal ribbed design, this was considered very up-to-date and modern, they were also available in mottled matt cellulose decorations and a wide range of pleasing shades.

In 1937 the ROPE series of vases and jardinieres was introduced, they had an overlapping ridged rope design, the numbers are 1306 to 1310, a new range of this design was produced in the 1950s and many numbers can be found between 2131 and 2320, the most popular colouring found in the later numbers was a white matt finish with a pale green top edge to the vases and jardinieres. Wire flower grids were also available with many jardinieres and can sometimes be found insitu. Unfortunately if these are left in the vases too long, rust marks on the inside can result.

Another early range was WILD DUCK which has an embossed flight of, usually, two ducks flying over bullrushes. This probably dates back to the 1920s when the numbers were in the 700s and

800s, (old Shaw & Copestake numbers), one piece, number **801** has a Registered Number 768695 which dates the original design as being entered in 1931 or 1932. There are earlier mould numbers in this range which include a clockset, numbers **649** and **650** but it is possible the clock shape was re-used for WILD DUCK a few years later with the wild duck pattern added, so one has to date by pattern rather than shape. I have left the researching of the early Shaw & Copestake ware to Anthony Van der Woerd who will no doubt enlighten us all with the answers to these tricky questions in due course. WILD DUCK pieces include dressing table sets, and table centres, mostly produced in the colourful cellulose finish. These were added to in the 1940s, numbers **1851** to 1860, when they were handpainted in a matt glaze, and also in a plain matt white. Some of the later pieces were also produced in the old cellulose type finish, but this style of finish was not to continue for much longer than the early 1950s. WILD DUCK included a lamp base which was similar to vase number 1857. Early WILD DUCK also had its own named green label, these pieces are considered very collectable especially if the cellulose finish is in good condition.

MISTY MORN vases were first produced in the Thomas Lawrence factory in the late 1940s. The blue colour was actually a cobalt blue clay body, only used at the Thomas Lawrence factory, the original MISTY MORN was a hand painted aerographed stencilled pattern. The numbers are F221, F223, F226, F249, F259, F260, F272, Collon vase, Crescent basket, Hudson fruit bowl, Chang No 1 and Regal number 2 vases. These shapes were also used with other decorations. MISTY MORN was re-introduced at the Shaw & Copestake factory in the 1970s using a blue glaze, lithographs and only a small amount of aerograph. The numbers used were F196 to F199, F223, vase 3064, plate 3261, tray 4198, tankard 4254. The difference in the quality and colour of the blue has been remarked on by collectors, and you will probably notice the difference between the original F223 and a re-introduced one. But it is an interesting piece of information from Mr. E. Roy Taylor former Works Director of Shaw & Copestake.

A similar re-introduction was carried out with CAVALIER. The original CAVALIER made in the Falcon Ware factory, was hand painted on embossed shapes. The numbers are F300, F304 to F307, F309, F313, 1774, 1775 and 1801. When it was re-introduced in the 1970s at the Shaw & Copestake factory the heavy embossment was removed and lithographs and a little aerograph shading was used. The numbers of the later CAVALIER are 5325 to 5333, it was then called NEW CAVALIER. There can be no mistaking the difference in the two designs, and obviously the earlier CAVALIER first produced in the Thomas Lawrence factory is much sought after.

IVY WARE, was very popular and is often found today in matt colours of green, fawn and sometimes white, a bright green glossy glaze was also produced at a later date. There is a very large range of IVY WARE and the numbers are scattered between 2027 and **2651**. The most unusual piece of IVY WARE is the dish with handle number 2039 3½" high, which is most delightful. There is also a cheese dish number 2088 and a dish with a lid number 2089, so as well as many flower and plant pots a few tableware pieces were produced. I know a lot of SylvaC collectors are devotees of IVY WARE which has a very solid and reliable feel to it. It was discontinued sometime in the 1960s.

AUTUMN, a small range of bulb bowls, flower pots, jardinieres and a wall vase with an embossed design of a spreading tree in autumn colours. Where applicable the handles are made to simulate tree branches. AUTUMN is very pleasing and not found too often as only a few pieces were designed, quite possibly not more than six different shapes. Numbers are 2114 to 2116, 2152, 2156, 2159, and were produced during the 1950s and 1960s. It was quite expensive to make due to the way the embossed pattern had to be carefully aerographed. AUTUMN should not be confused with the much later AUTUMN LEAVES, the pattern of which consisted of embossed leaves hand decorated in Autumn tints and a green glaze. This was produced in 1979, the numbers are 5499 to 5509, it was modelled by George Matthews, but was not widely distributed.

RAPHIQUE is a typical modern 1950s type design of vertical ridged lines, and is coloured in either red, black, yellow or green, with the vertical lines in white. The numbers are mainly from 2171 to 2192 with a few odd numbers outside that sequence. It is quite striking with each piece having a scalloped edge at the top, but otherwise straight lines. RAPHIQUE consists mostly of vases and flowerpots but there is a teapot number 2188 with a sugar bowl and cream jug, and also a cruet set. Similarly CHESTERFIELD also has ridged lines but set at a slight angle, the colours are lemon, lilac, stone and white in matt glazes. The edges are completely straight, with no extra embellishments, and all the pieces which are mainly flower pots and vases are completely plain. CHESTERFIELD dates slightly later than RAPHIQUE and was produced in the early 1960s, the numbers are scattered between 3031 and 3256.

The LACE range has many pieces which include a cheese dish, honey pot, tray and cruet, but most are flower containers. It has a lace effect embossed on each piece, which is picked out in white, and was available in black, maroon and yellow. I have a small sweet dish decorated with hand painted flowers, number 2223. The numbers are spread between **2212** and 2327, once again many of the edges of this series are scalloped. Although usually highly glazed, it was also produced in matt colours the raised lace effect showing through in a lighter colour.

Produced at the same time as LACE was CACTUS, numbering between 2209 and 2308, these were flower holders and plant pots with no tableware as far as I know. Each piece looks remarkably like a cactus, it was produced in green and fawn matt and glossy. One interesting feature of CACTUS is that there are two wall vases of different designs, number **2262** and 2293, this being the larger of the two.

I have never thought PLUME to be very exciting, it was available in three pastel colours, lilac, stone and yellow, each piece had four or so feathers embossed on the items in a contrasting colour. A few pieces of tableware were also available, and numbers are between 2385 and 2411. It was originally described as '*an enchanting design in three new pastel backgrounds*'.

NAUTILUS was described in the catalogue as '*yet another exciting new development of the already familiar "SHELL" designs.*' It has all the obvious hallmarks of SylvaC, the vases are quite extraordinary, almost defying description. To me, they look like waves, leaning to one side, the tops and bases also have wavy edges, and the middle of the vases have vertical ridges. On looking up the word nautilus I find it is described as – *a type of shell* – and certainly number F724 in the range is a good representation. The other numbers are F726, F753, F756, 2439 to 2441 and 2449. The most popular colours were white matt with pale green shading inside. They were produced between the 1950s and 1960s, and are rarely seen.

MOSELLE was modelled by Mr. Reginald Thompson, and his favourite, he loved the little cupid, although of the ten pieces designed only seven actually incorporated the little chap. Moselle meaning – *a dry white wine produced near the Moselle river in Germany* – must surely have grapes incorporated into the design somewhere and most of the pieces do in fact have them. The numbers are scattered between 2465 and 2783, the cupid pieces are usually in white matt, although some can be found in blended yellows, blues and greens and are most attractive. I have a lovely jardiniere, 2474, which is half yellow and half green and the effect is very pleasing. MOSELLE was first produced in the 1950s with some pieces still being made in 1982.

The all time favourite HYACINTH LEAF has numbers ranging between 2321 and 2489 and even a much later number 4132, which was a fern pot. It had no tableware, but consisted of vases, flowerpots, jardinieres, bowls, posy troughs and a wall vase. It was a SylvaC best seller, and produced from the late 1950s until 1982. Each piece is incised to represent hyacinth leaves, and was available in deep shiny green, matt fawn, white, yellow and turquoise. Many people collect HYACINTH LEAF, the white pieces considered the most desirable. Probably the simple elegance of the design attracts collectors. It was produced for many years and is quite plentiful, no doubt there are many homes with at least one HYACINTH LEAF vase still being put to good use.

LARONDE is very plain with vertical stripes in white, on a background of black, deep green or salmon. There are a few pieces of tableware to be found, such as a cheese dish and cruet set. I have seen the cheese dish for sale at a high price and described as Art Deco, well, I can only assume it to be 1960s Art Deco! The numbers are scattered between 2567 and 2638, perhaps it will become collectable in later years as it is a typical 1960s style, when it was mainly produced, various pieces are often seen for sale.

BAMBOO is, as it suggests, styled as bamboo shoots. This has under twenty pieces, and is mostly found in a bamboo colour but also in green and fawn matt colours and even mottled shades. It is not seen too often, and was probably not popular at the time. The numbers are spread between 2740 and **2816**, it was one of the many ranges produced in the 1960s. It was redesigned in 1977 and re-numbered 5369 to 5379, when it proved more popular, and produced until 1982.

APPLE BLOSSOM also produced in the 1960s and 1970s is very attractive. The Apple Blossom is embossed on each piece which is handpainted in natural colours on a mottled background with a satin finish. The decoration is so lifelike it really does bring a breath of Spring to your home. The numbers of this range are scattered between 2870 and 2937.

MAGNOLIA is also beautifully styled, each piece actually being in the shape of a magnolia flower, with leaves and twigs incorporated into the base, or handles in the case of the jardiniere. The flowers are white matt with delicate pink shading, and hand painted bases. There is even a MAGNOLIA cup and saucer number 3547, which was modelled by Mr. Woolham. The other numbers are spread between 2954 and 3218, it was produced during the 1960s and 1970s. A very collectable series, which tends towards the expensive.

Many collectors are keen on LILY, and it has to be said the pieces are beautifully modelled. The lily is usually white tinged with yellow, and the leaves green with a matt finish. There are about twelve items in this set, which was produced during the 1960s, the numbers are spread between 3101 and 3292. Although I am named Susan which means Lily, I cannot bring myself to have any examples of LILY at home as they give me a feeling of great morbidity.

MARINA and PEBBLE are frequently seen, and have differing effects upon collectors. PEBBLE is cleverly modelled, by Reginald Thompson and John Lawson, each piece looks as if it is covered with different coloured pebbles. MARINA modelled by Reginald Thompson, is a similar style but covered with varying types of shells, which is very realistic. Both MARINA and PEBBLE were popular and have endured through the years well, they are solid, well made and can be bought for reasonable prices. PEBBLE numbers range between 3349 and 3482, a lamp base is number 3683, it was produced during the 1960s and 1970s. MARINA was also produced during this time, the numbers are 4152 to 4163. The quality of painting was most important as each pebble or shell was individually coloured. If you study a piece of MARINA you will appreciate the amount of work involved in the decorating.

I am grateful to collectors who have sent details of vases from ranges such as a Looped, Lattice, Fern, Oak, Fuchsia, the Alpine pattern with rope seams, and the Chequers pattern. Other SylvaC ranges include Tudor, which has an incised pattern, the Slymcraft vases, Palm, Wall pattern, Privet, Coral, Linton, Begonia, Texture, Oslo, Manhatten, Maple, Olympus, Flora, Aurora, Sycamore, Agincourt, Harmony, Appolo, Rhapsody, Spectrum, Etruscan, Fleur, Banana leaf range, Gossamer range, Vintage range, etc., etc. There is a list of new numbers received from collectors at the back of this book.

You can see from the above there was considerable productivity at the SylvaC factory during the 1960s and 1970s. Not content with keeping to the same designs, new ones were constantly being produced supplanting the old, with a few old faithfuls like HYACINTH LEAF continuing throughout the years. There will always be many SylvaC vases to collect for sometime to come, as they are still in everyday use in homes throughout the Country if not the World.

▲ Shell design. Page from a SylvaC catalogue c.1936/1937.

▼ Shell design. Low numbers are Falcon numbers.

▲ Page from a SylvaC catalogue c.1936/1937.

▼ Misty Morn range. From a SylvaC catalogue c.1980. Low numbers are Falcon numbers.

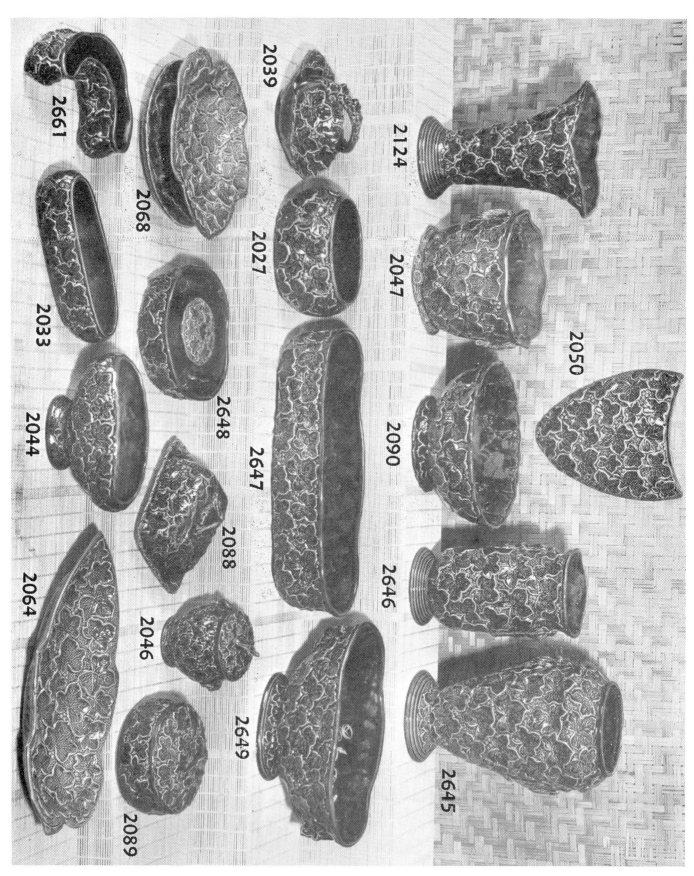

2661

2068

2039

2124

2033

2027

2047

2050

2648

2647

2090

2646

2044

2088

2064

2046

2649

2645

2089

▲ Ivy range. From a SylvaC catalogue.

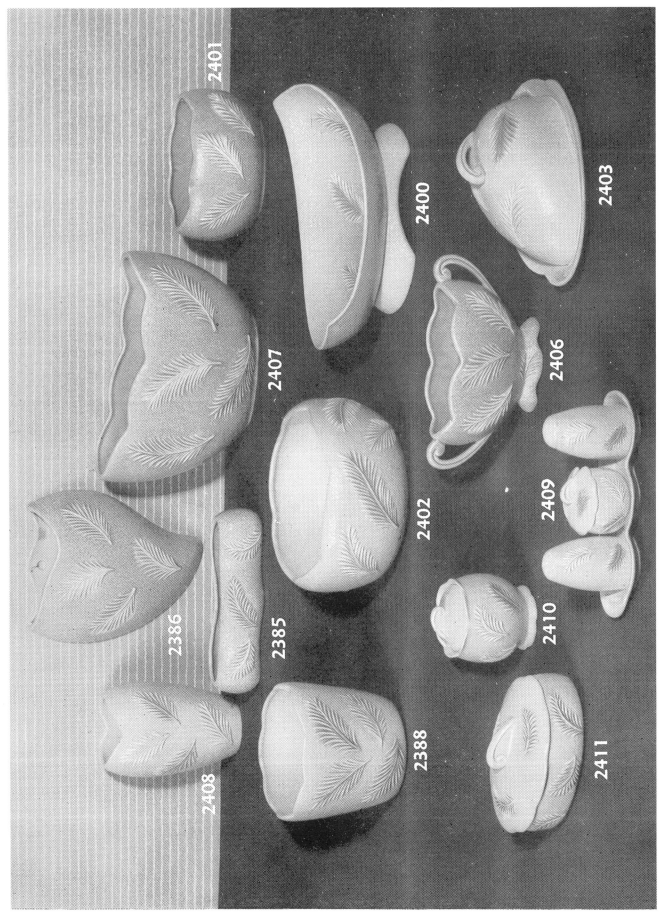

▲ Plume range.

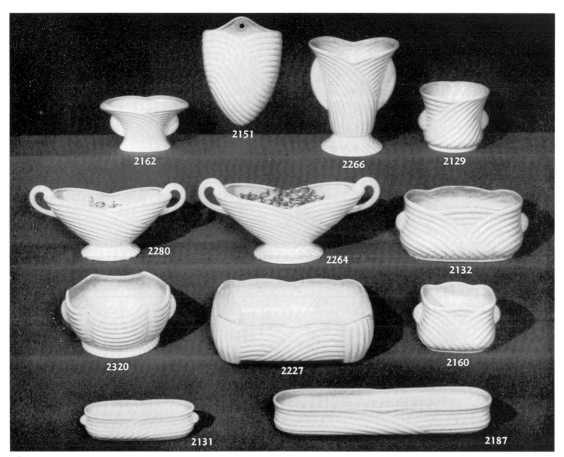

2162 2151 2266 2129

2280 2264 2132

2320 2227 2160

2131 2187

▲ Rope range.

▼ Nautilus range. Low numbers are Falcon numbers.

2441 2449 2439 726 724

2440 753 756

▲ Cellulose patterns. From a SylvaC catalogue c.1936/1937.

▼ Hyacinth range.

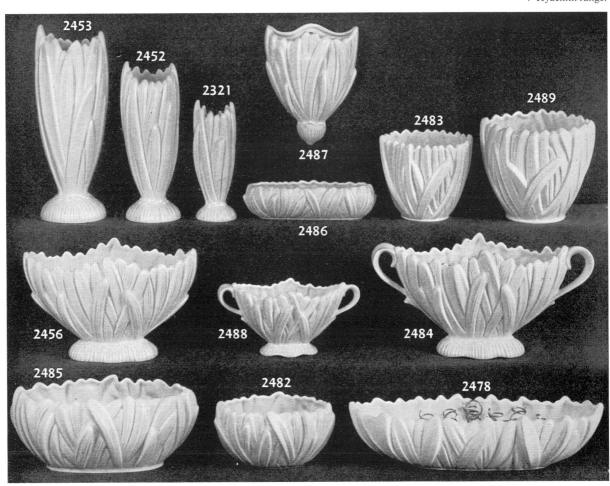

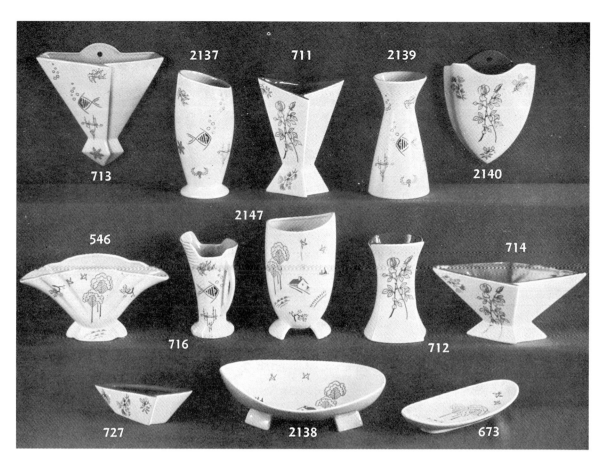

▲ Aqua, Gronant and Rose decorations.   ▼ Duotone range.

▲ Left: Jardiniere 2122, centre: Jardiniere number 2499, right: Basket jug 2373.

▼ Sablon range.

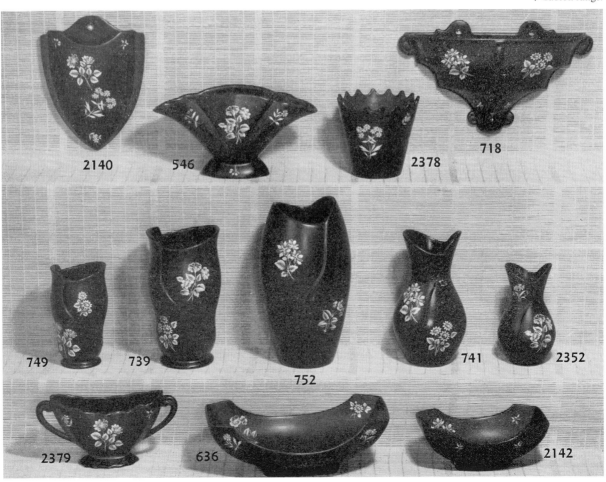

2875

2937

2883

2876

2874

2882

2878

2885

2884

2872

2877

2870

▲ Apple Blossom range. Hand painted on a mottled background with a matt finish.

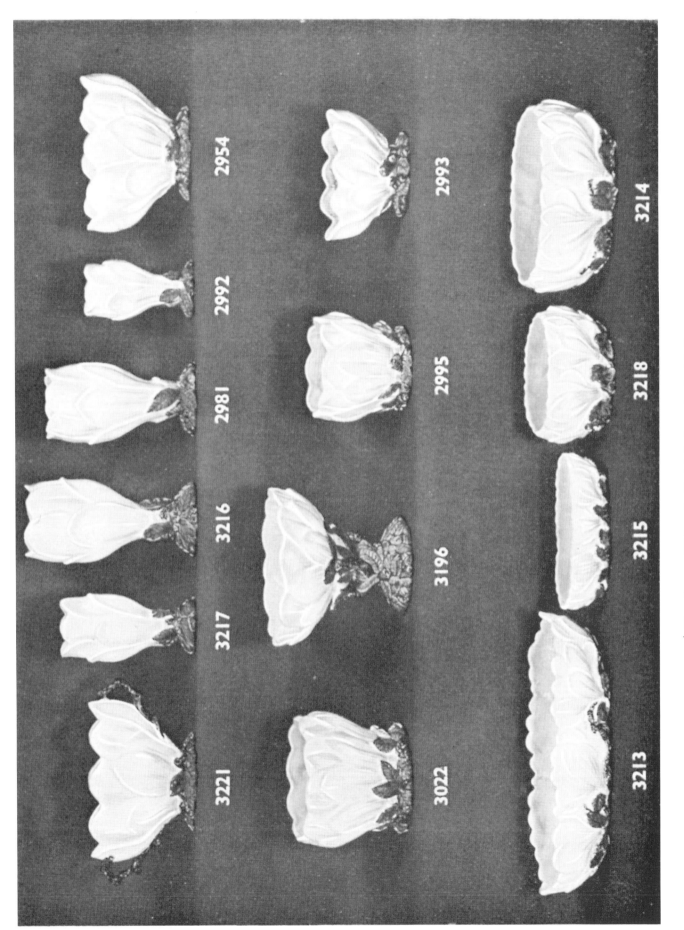

2954 2992 2981 3216 3217 3221

2993 2995 3196 3022

3214 3218 3215 3213

▲ Magnolia range. White matt with pink shading on hand painted base.

5270/Hide　　**5271/Hide**　　**5281/Hide**

▲ Leather covered tankards.

▼ Slymcraft range.

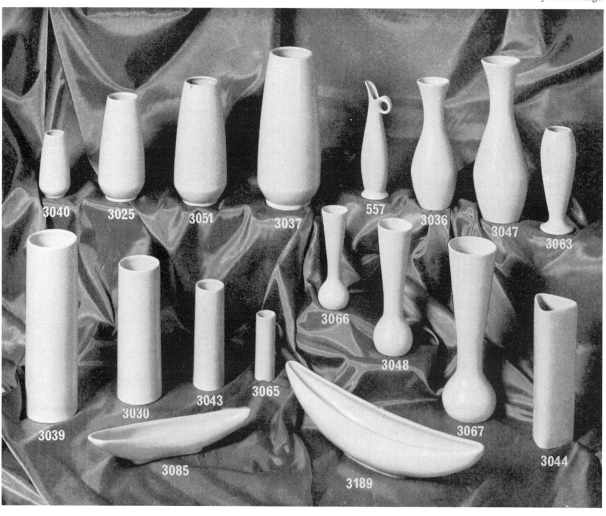

76

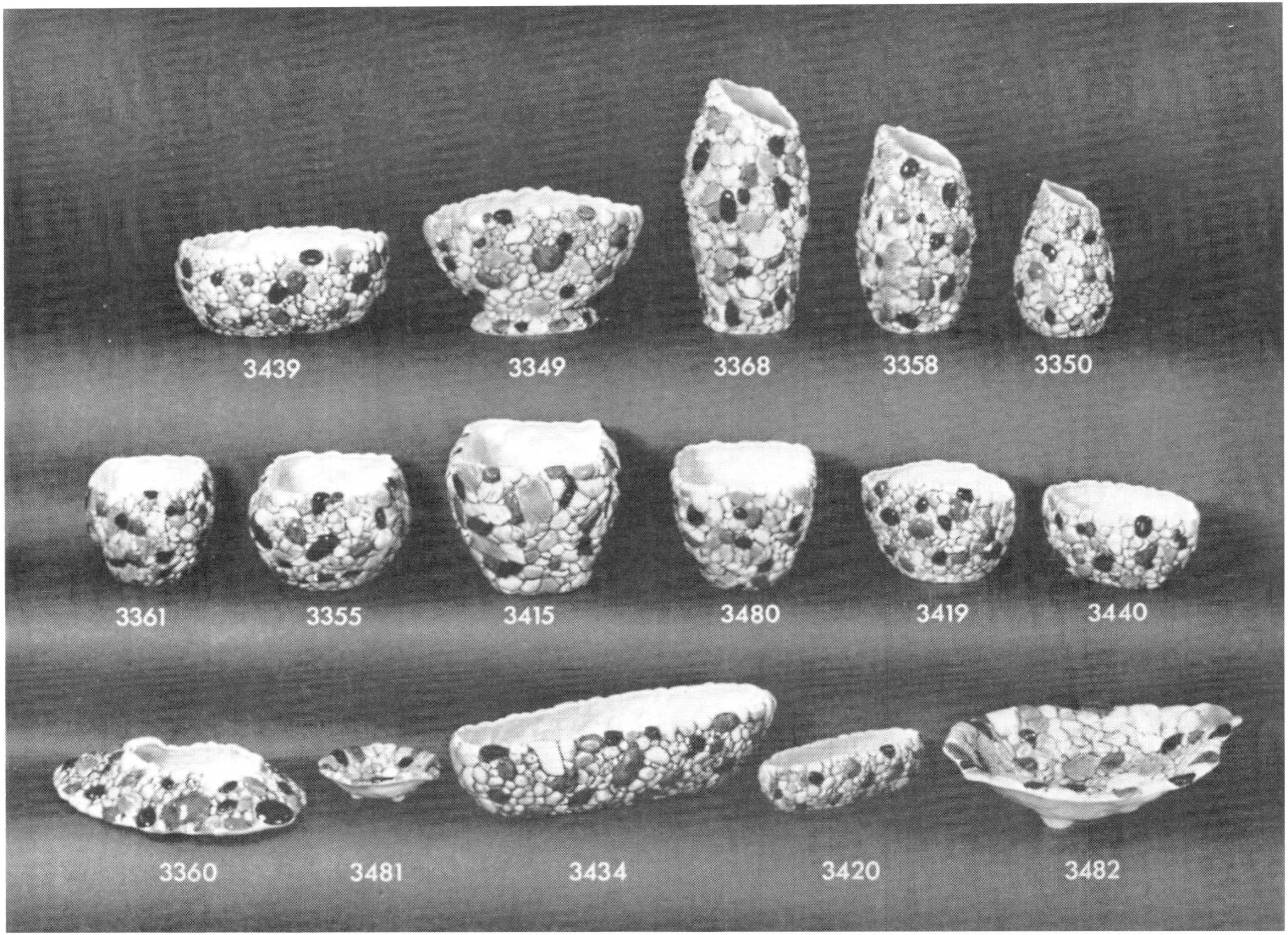

3350

3358

3368

3349

3439

3440

3419

3480

3415

3355

3361

3482

3420

3434

3481

3360

▲ Pebbles range. Hand painted.

77

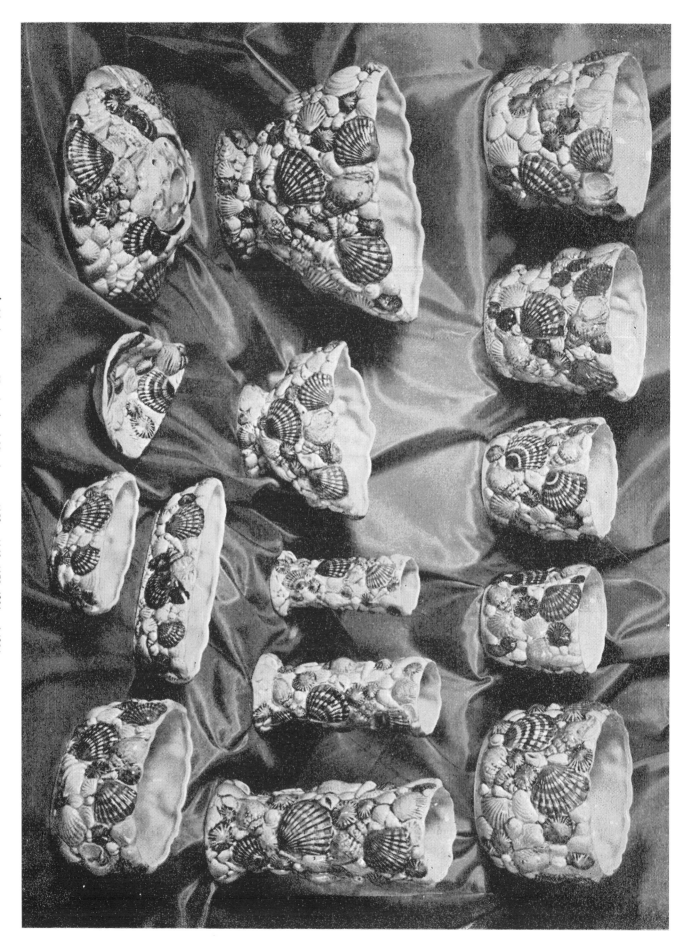

▲ Marina range: Hand painted. Numbers are 4152 to 4163, 4178, 4201 and 4204.

2626

2562

2683

2474

2465

2729

2564

2566

2783

▲ Moselle range.

79

▲ Olympus range.

4103
4098
4130
4093
4105
4115
4086
4084
4131
4080
3998
4081

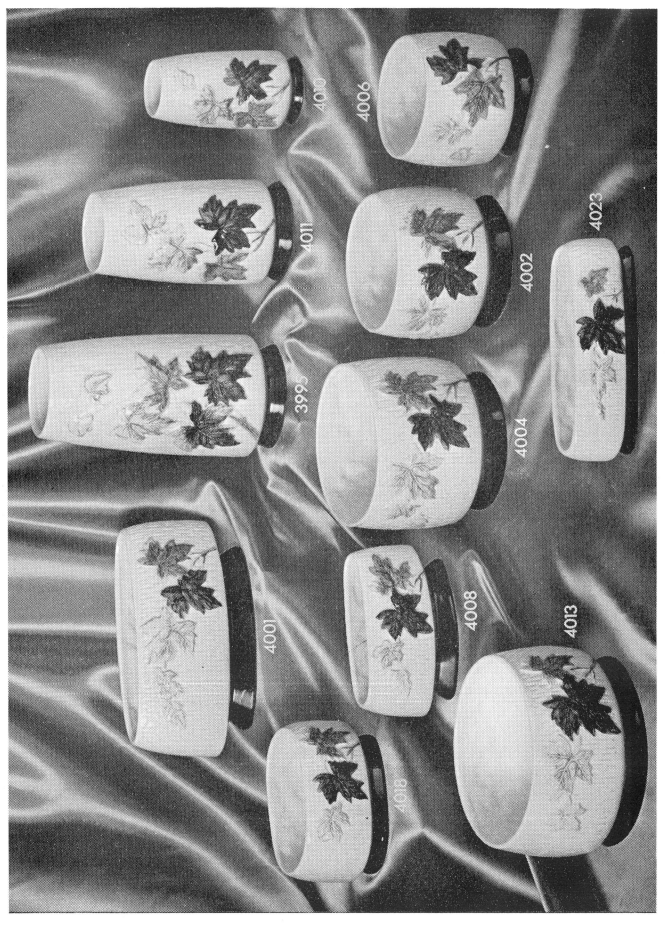

▲ Maple range.

▲ Flora range.

4174

4168

4164

4171

4165

4166

4170

4173

4172

4169

4212

4209

4207

4211

4210

4129

4208

4206

4205

4214

4213

4215

4127

▲ Sycamore range.

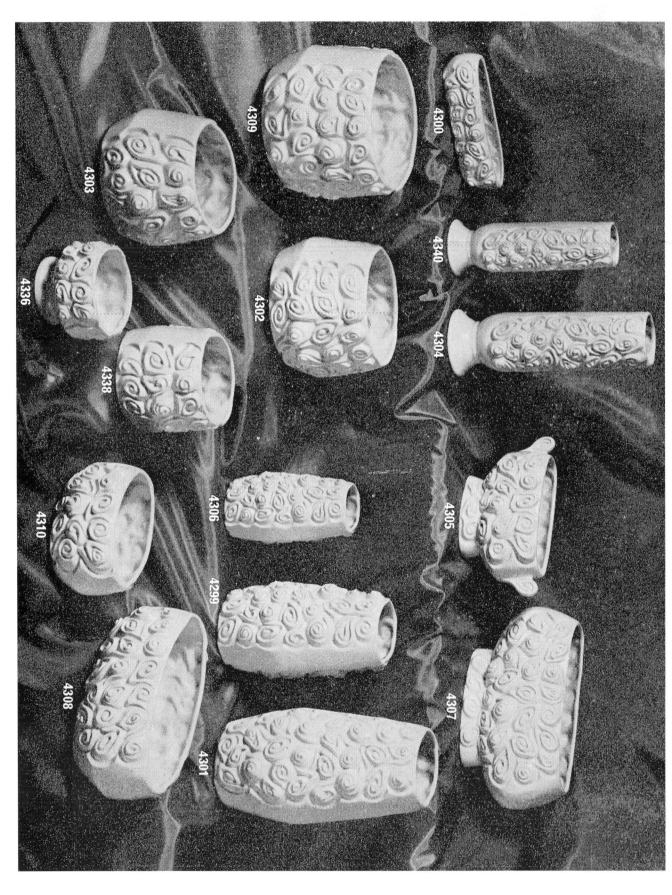

▲ Harmony range.

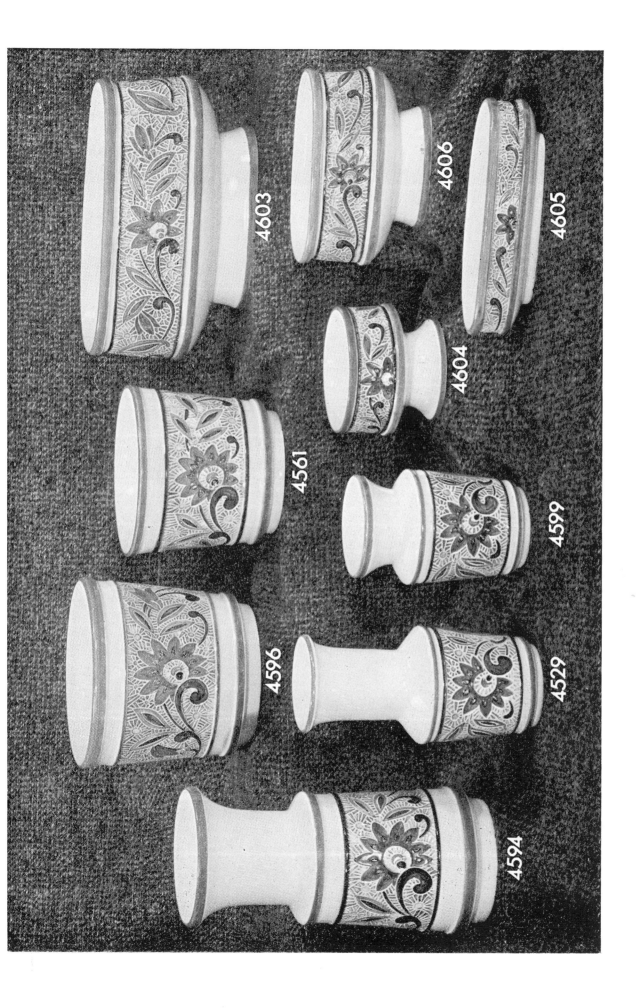

4603

4606

4605

4604

4561

4599

4596

4529

4594

▲ Gossamer range.

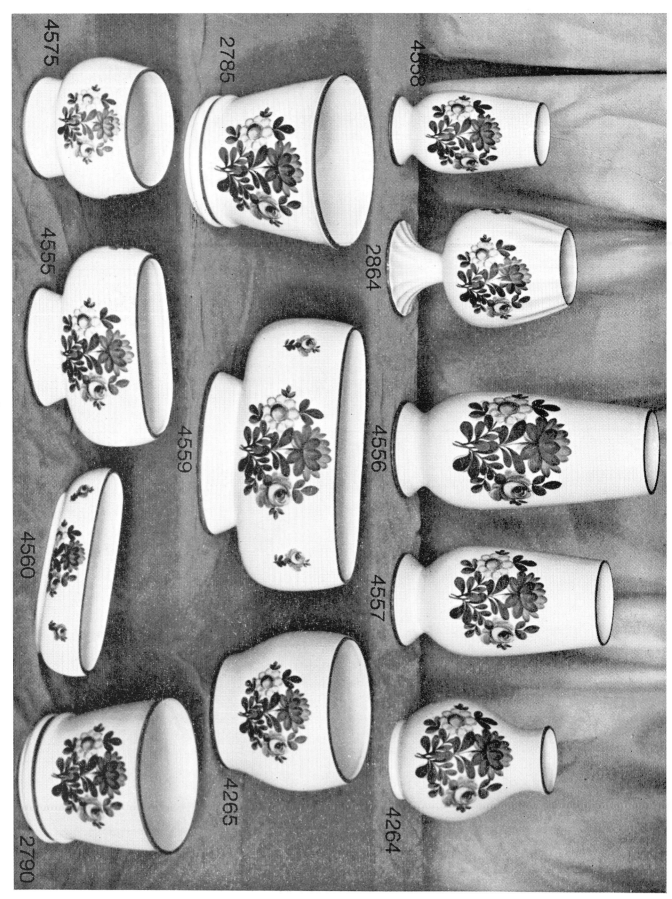

4575
2785
4558
2864
4555
4559
4556
4557
4560
4265
4264
2790

▲ Autumn Chintz.

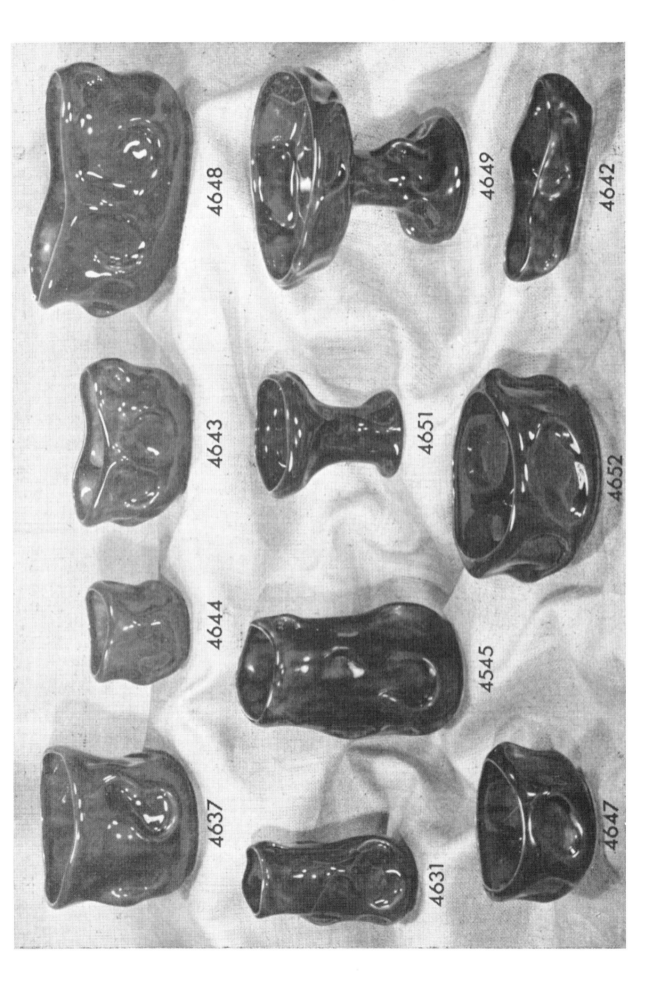

4648

4649

4642

4643

4651

4652

4644

4545

4637

4631

4647

▲ Spectrum range.

87

4613   4526   4612

4666   4608   4554   4638

4641   4645   4665   4620

▲ Rhapsody range.   ▼ Aurora range.

4323   4324   4325

4330

4328   4319   4327   4329

4331

4195   4197   4198

4244   4196

3996/Suede

3632/Suede

4009/Suede

▲ Suede covered tankard and ashtrays.

▼ Etruscan range.

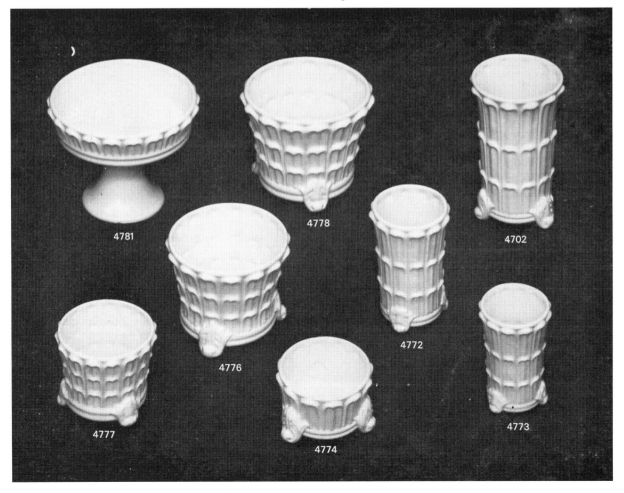

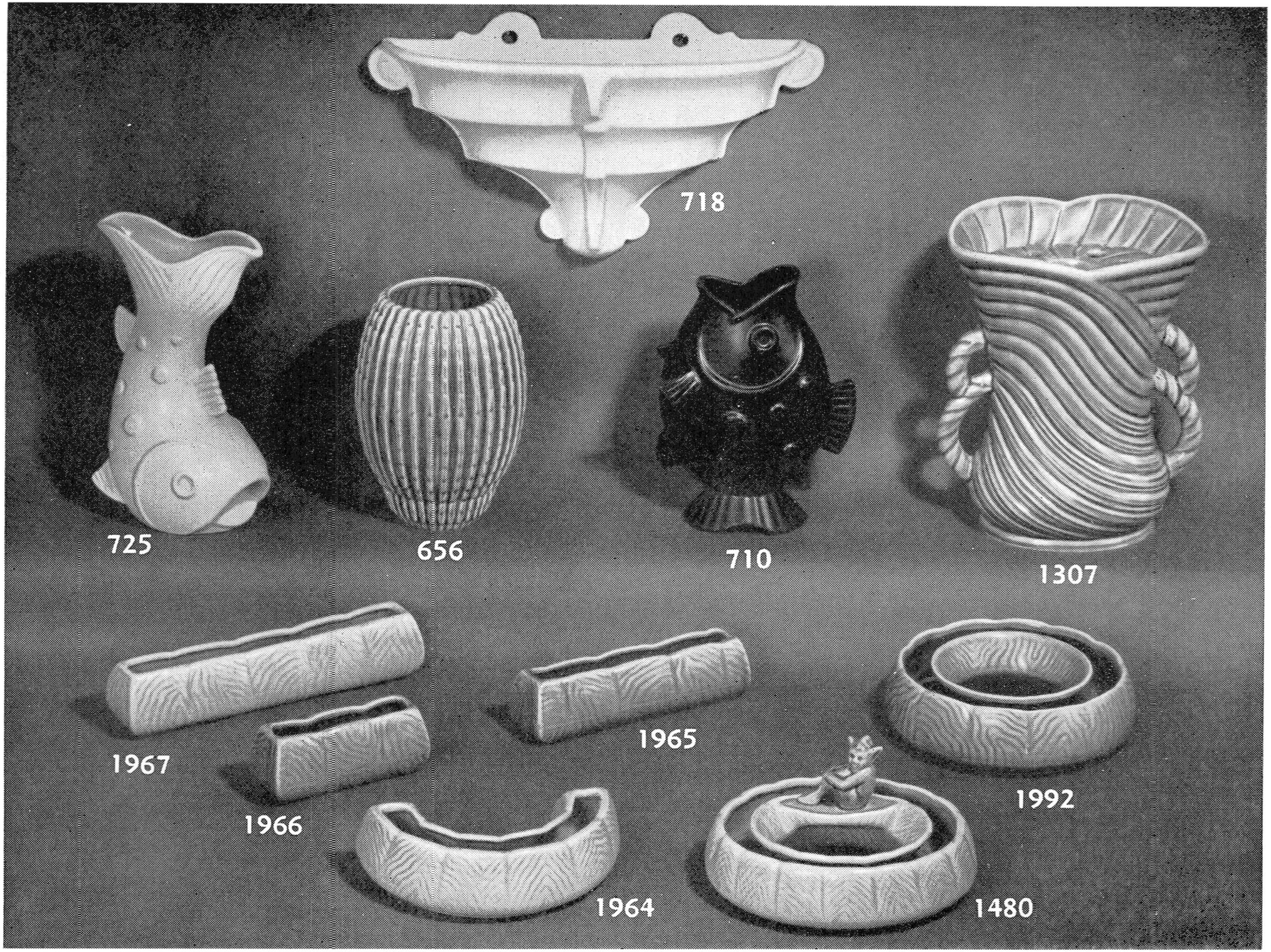

▲ Page from a SylvaC catalogue. Low numbers are Falcon numbers.

725
1967
1966
656
718
1964
1965
710
1480
1992
1307

▲ Classic range, Falcon numbers.

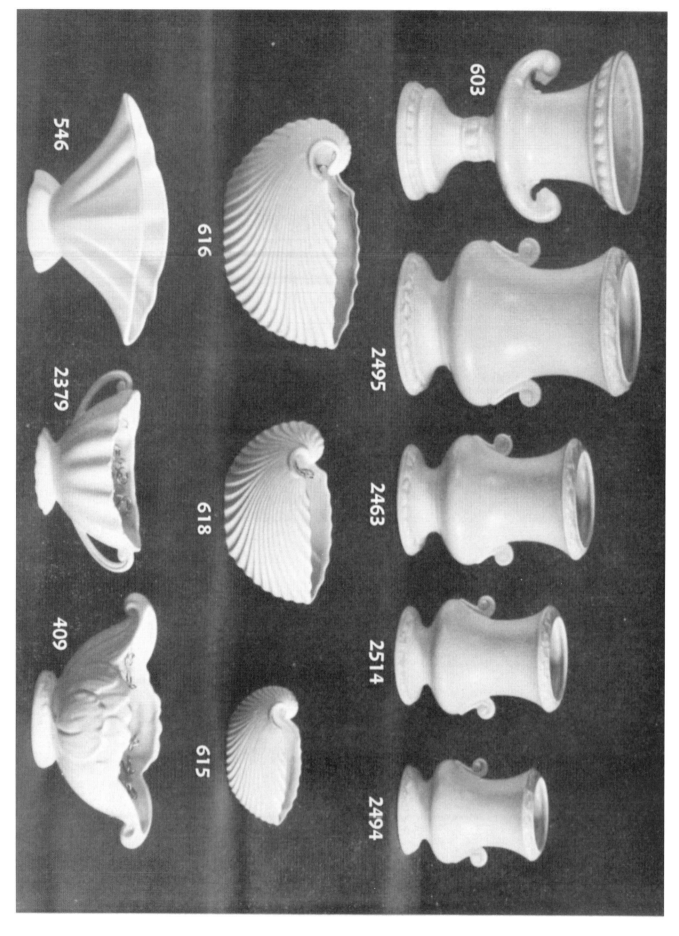

603   2495   2463   2514   2494

546   616

2379   618

409   615

▲ Urns and Jardinieres. Low numbers are Falcon numbers.

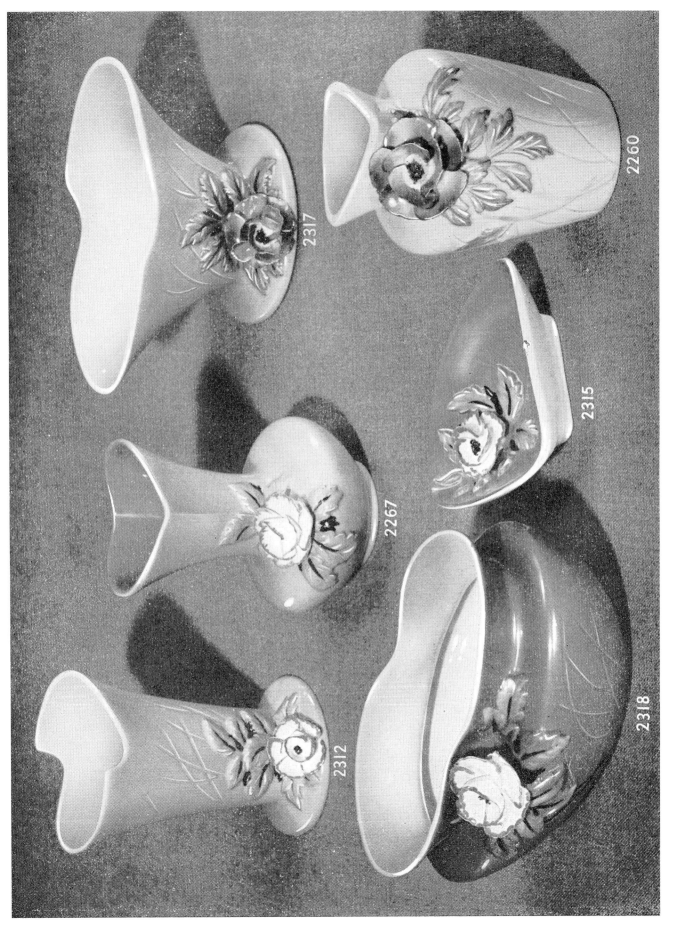

▲ New Style Floral.

2317

2260

2315

2267

2312

2318

▲ Vases from a SylvaC catalogue c.1980. Low numbers are Falcon numbers.

▼ Milady range.

5393 5398 5394

5395 5397 5399 5396

▲Canton range.　　　▼Bamboo range.

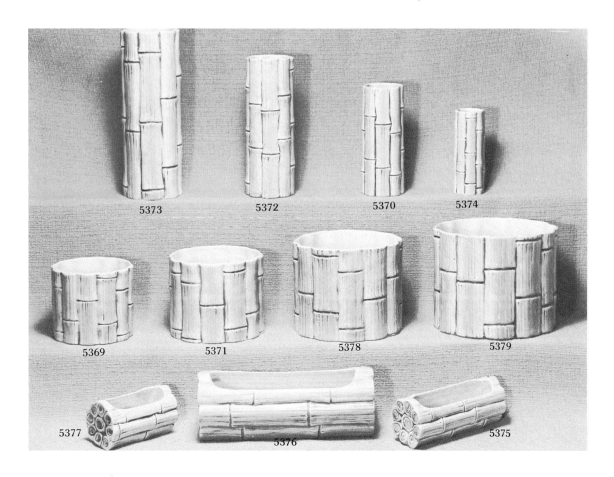

5373 5372 5370 5374

5369 5371 5378 5379

5377 5376 5375

Belgravia Range *by* SYLVAC ERAMICS

Fresh as the gently falling snow in the winter countryside, the clean, 'china' white finish on this pattern is a delightful medium for flowers. The cache-pots, carefully made to suit popular sizes of plant pots, are ideal covers to grace any decor.

▲ Complete page from an original SylvaC catalogue.

3844   4535   4537   3624   3842

3896   3895   4536   4539   4540

▲ Privet range.   ▼ Hollington range.

5471   5470   5476   5473   5469   5475   5474   5472

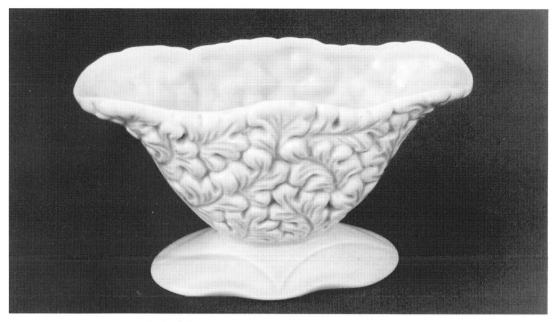

▲ Jardinière number 2991 7½" long oak leaf design. From the collection of and photograph by Mr. J. Roberts.

▲ Vase number 4695 6½" high, colour brown and white. From the collection of Mr. K.A. Huckstep. Photograph by John Symonds.

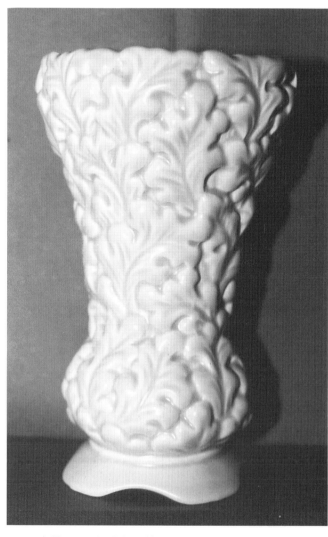

▲ Vase number 2927 8" high oak leaf design. From the collection of and photograph by Mr. & Mrs. R. Walker.

▲ Jardiniere number 2894 about 7″ long. From the
collection of and photograph by Mr. & Mrs. R. Walker.

▲ Vase 2505 15″ high. From the collection of John Howard.
Photograph by Neil France.

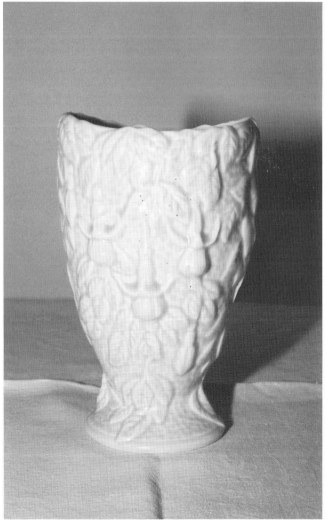

▲ Vase number 3269 7¾″ high Fuschia range. From the
collection of and photograph by Mrs. Ann Newman.

▲ Jardiniere number 2817 6¾″ long. Lattice range. From the collection of Mr. K. Huckstep. Photogragh by John Symonds.

▲ Vase number 2712 10″ long, looped design, green matt. From the collection of and photograph by Judith Cox-Rogers.

▲ Vase number 3460 10″ high Seahorse range. From the collection of and photograph by Mrs. Jane Hallsworth.

Jug 426 6"h
Jug 427 9¼"h

Jug 260 8"h
Jug 259 10"h
Jug 272 12"h

Alex No.2 9½"h
Alex No.1 11½"h

Jug 1824 8¼"h

Jug 562 6½"h

Jug 1344 9"h

Jug 1409 5¼"h
Jug 1410 8"h

Jug 393 3"h
Jug 1970 5¼"h

Jug 1971 5¼"h
Jug 394 3"h

Jug 1685 7"h

Jug 1782 6½"h
Jug 1655 8"h

Jug 1342 6¼"h

Jug 386 8"h

Jug 1418 8¼"h

Jug 1404 6½"h

Jug 1175 6¼"h

Jug 1625 6"h

Jug 1367 6"h

Jug 1623 6"h

Jug 1745 6"h

Jug 561 4½"h

All three figure numbers are Falcon numbers.

Jug 486 10½"h

Jug 571 8¼"h

Jug 564 9"h

Jug 463 5¼"h

Jug 557 7¼"h

Jug 1253 6"h

Jug 1795 6"h

Jug 426 6"h
Jug 427 9¼"h

Jug 1784 6¼"h

Jug 1794 7"h 7"l

Vase 1578 8"h

Vase 196 7½"h

Vase 1758 6"h

Vase 385 8¼"h

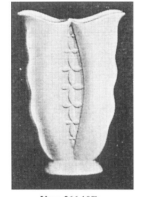

Vase 566 10"h

Vase 1807 9¾"h

Vase 626 7"h

Vase 380 8"h

All three figure numbers are Falcon numbers.

Vase 684 5"h
Vase 1343 9"h

Vase 1833 8½"h

Vase 1835 8½"h

Vase 1836 8½"h

Vase 258 10"h

Vase 1831 6½"h

Vase 1832 8¼"h

Vase 623 7"h

Vase 1834 8½"h

Vase 383 10"h

Vase 1837 8½"h

Vase 387 8¼"h

Vase 1407 8½"h

Vase 675 5"h
Vase 1571 8½"h

Vase 1570 7"h

Vase 1575 6"h

All three figure numbers are Falcon numbers.

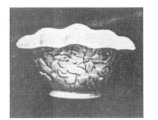

Bowl 1653
9¼"l 5½"h

Bowl 1783
6½"l 4"h

Empress vase
7¾"h

Chang No.1 vase
8½"h

Bowl 409 9½" across
Falcon number

Diamond basket with
grid 898 10"l 5¼"h

Diamond bowl with
grid 1826 7"l 5"h

York Vase
14¾"h

Vase 1786 4½"h

Vase 1538 3½"h

Spill Vase 1271 5"h

Vase 1490 4¾"h

Vase 1491 4¾"h

Bulb Bowl 1827
5½"l 3½"h

Ginger jar and
cover 14"h

Cigarette Box
4"×1¼"×2"

Ash tray

Vase 1732 9"h

Vase 1787 4¼"h

All three figure numbers are Falcon numbers.

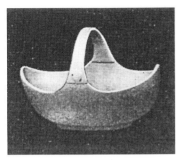

Basket 1796
6¼"l 4½"h

Basket 1777
3½"h

Basket 1780
5½"h

Bon Bon basket
1829 9"l

Crescent basket
12" across

Bowl 494 3¼"h

Sweet 1791 6¼"l 2¼"h

Sweet 1654 5"l 2"h

Wall vase 1395
6¼"h

Bowl 287 10" across

Floral tray 13"l

Hudson tray
10½" diameter

Bulb bowl 1830 8½"l

Crescent boat 12" across

Bowl 252 12" diameter

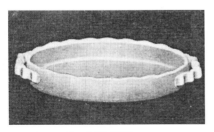

Bowl 493 11½"l

Flower holder 494 3¼"h

Bowl 485 5½"h

All three figure numbers are Falcon numbers.

MR. SYLVAC INTRODUCES THE HOUSEWIFE AND SYLVAC

I know vase collectors will be most interested in a booklet produced by Shaw & Copestake, probably in the 1960s, devoted to the art of flower arranging. It was called 'Mr. SylvaC introduces the housewife and SylvaC', the following text and photographs are taken from this booklet which was designed and produced at the Buxton Press.

Introduction

It may be as yet you are unfamiliar with the name of 'SylvaC', in which case permit us to introduce ourselves as manufacturers of ornamental pottery and tableware. Those to whom our products are already well-known, will tell you that we manufacture one of the most extensive ranges of high quality Vases, Flower Bowls, Animal Figures and Novelties, Table Accessories etc., available today. They are all British made, too.

The following pages are principally devoted to the Floral arrangement aspect of 'SylvaC' ware. We hope that this booklet will give our friends, both old and new, further ideas for putting that 'something extra' into the home.

The Housewife and SylvaC

In these days of the flower-conscious housewife, there is an ever increasing demand for attractive Bowls and Vases in which to display flowers. So much so that we have decided to publish this booklet showing typical arrangements in some of the containers now available in the 'SylvaC' range.

The illustrations show a wide variety of ideal shapes in settings such as may be found in many homes, throughout the world – may be your home. Here, we, as manufacturers appreciate, not only the necessity of good shape design, but also that the decoration must blend with the decor of the home and at the same time not clash with the flowers. We find that although White Matt and Black Matt are still the most popular colours for the flower arranger, decorated Bowls, such as our 'Pebbles' pattern now command much attention in this field.

Some useful hints particularly for the beginner

Whilst many of the deeper type of 'SylvaC' Bowls are supplied with special wire flower-holders, if these are not available there are now other types of holders readily obtainable at Departmental Stores, Florists, etc. On the other hand a crumpled piece of wire netting such as chicken netting is a good substitute. Care should be taken in crumpling the netting so that the stems of the flowers can pass through several thicknesses. For the lower type of Bowl and Tray, pin-holders make the best foundation for your arrangements, in some cases it may help to secure these holders with plasticine, in order to make your arrangement more stable.

Before arranging your flowers cut off the ends of the stems with a sharp knife or scissors. In the case of hard-wooded stems, such as, Roses, Lilac, etc., it is better to crush the base of the stem with a hammer to make them last longer. Then, if possible, stand your flowers over-night in a bucket of cold water ensuring that the water comes well up the stems.

Consider carefully how you are going to arrange the flowers before starting and give yourself plenty of time. In this way you can have every confidence that you will make a great success of your floral arrangement.

If you have any difficulty, no doubt your local Floral Arrangement Society, of which there is at least one in most of the Towns and Cities throughout the British Isles, will be pleased to advise you.

Always remember that flowers live longest in ordinary room temperature. Avoid draughts and excessive heat from the fire, radiator or the sun. Do not change the water in the container, but keep it well filled.

◀ This bowl (3189) in Black Matt finish is an excellent shape for a narrow shelf or mantelpiece. Here it is seen arranged with a single Arum Lily, but on the other hand it looks equally as well with a selection of multi-coloured small flowers. This 'SylvaC' Horse (15) completes the setting.

▲ For the more ambitious flower arranger this low 'Opelle' Bowl (3465) offers the widest scope. In this illustration the tall Iris have been supplemented with Eucalyptus Leaves around the base of the arrangement. A corner table makes a fine setting. The model Cairn Terrier (3447) lends additional attraction to the scene.

▲ When it comes to potted plants what better Flower Pot Holder that this item (3415) from the 'Pebbles' range. Delightfully coloured in the natural Black, Brown, Grey and Fawn of real pebbles it lends beauty to any plant in the home.

▲ Arranged tastefully with a single red Poinsettia and trailing Ivy, this 'Opelle' Wall Vase (3466) in a White Matt finish adds much to the decor of your lounge, dining room or hall. The caricature Siamese Cats (large size 3457 and small size 3404) are amongst the most recent additions to the 'SylvaC' animal range.

▼ A 'SylvaC' Flower Holder 3360 in 'Pebble' decoration simply but effectively arranged with Freesias supplemented by Cupressus branches from the garden.

▼ For an alcove, what better than this fine collection of 'SylvaC' animals which includes Elephants (large size 68, small size 92), Osprey (3339), Otter (3459), Pekinese (3165), Cairn (3447), Horses (3180 White and 15) and the set of Chimpanzees. These fine pieces either collectively or individually would do more than justice to any home.

▲ Daffodils, Tulips and Iris go together in the simple-to-arrange 'Opelle' Jardiniere (3341). This Jardiniere, too, is supplied with or without wire flower holder.

▲ The 'Sea Horse' Vase (3414) makes a splendid companion for the telephone. Arranged here with Tulips, Carnations and Eucalyptus Leaves. This is the very thing you need to brighten that spot in the room, which looks as though it requires something, but you are not quite sure what it is.

▼ Pink Carnations and small Larch branches make another exciting table top arrangement in a Tudor Vase (3492). This floral display has its own admirer in the form of a model Corgi (3128).

◄ Vase (3368) again from our 'Pebbles' range is shown here arranged with Iris, Carnations and Twigs from the garden. This vase by reason of its colour looks equally well with an arrangement of leaves and small branches, thus avoiding the use of flowers, which is particularly useful at times of the year when flowers are in short supply. Also in the picture is our graceful White Horse (3180).

◀ Using a smart plain White Matt Jardiniere (3225), against a window background with the garden beyond, a most attractive display can be achieved with Spring flowers supplemented by Ruskus. This Jardiniere or Flower Bowl can be supplied with special wire flower holder to assist the arranger.

To the well-initiated flower arranger this 'Sea Horse' Bowl ▶ (3370), presents a most exciting challenge. Seen here with Carnations and Ruskus this bowl is ideally designed to give the finest floral displays. The comical Mule (3383) is a popular item from the 'SylvaC' caricature animal range.

Although this "Hyacinth Leaf" Vase (2453) and Swan Holder (1127)
are the last items illustrated in this booklet, by no means do they represent
the end of the "SylvaC" story. The extent of the range of ornamental
pottery items available is far too large for the pages available here.
Therefore, the next time you think of buying a gift for a friend or treating
yourself to something special ask to see our range at the nearest
Pottery Shop or Department but
BE SURE TO ASK FOR "SYLVAC" WARE.

on sale where you see **"Mr. SylvaC"**

SHAW & COPESTAKE LTD.
Sylvan Works, Longton, Stoke-on-Trent
Telephone: 33037/8

Designed and produced at the Buxton Press

NOVELTY WARE

By novelty ware I mean ranges with animals attached or jugs and vases made into novel shapes. The lazy pixie series is a good example, and was very popular, the numbers are toadstool F707, wheelbarrow F708, log 2275, basket 2276, watering can 2277, flower pot 2278. But the lazy pixie is also found attached to other items and other characters can also be found on the above numbers. For instance I have seen toadstool F707 with several different additions such as gnome, dog, and mother rabbit who is a refugee from The House in the Glen range.

Several collectors have also mentioned little pot number **1996**, which usually has a small dog standing on his hind legs looking into it. It has been seen with the hippo, elephant or giraffe which are usually found on the palm tree vase number 2430. Another collector has a barrel type container number **2509** with the black cat usually seen on the chimney vase number 2425. All these slightly unusual additions are very collectable, and possibly quite rare.

Although the squirrel and acorn jugs or vases are frequently seen, I was interested to see a smaller version, which was introduced during the 1950s, number F**330**, which is only 6½″ high. Only one collector has so far come forward with this information, and it is not mentioned in any catalogues or adverts that I have seen, so I think this is extremely rare. There are seven different acorn and squirrel flower jugs to collect, numbers F**330**, **1115, 1195,** 1958, 1959, 4068 and miniature 1993.

I have come across handpainted examples of the acorn flower jug, which is very unusual and effective. The hollyhock flower jug number 1274 has also been found handpainted, with coloured hollyhocks, leading to some speculation as to whether they were handpainted outside the factory. It is known that in later years the factory did supply dipped white pieces which were then sold to outside decorating shops.

This idea of making flower vases or jugs incorporating an animal was well underway before World War II, with one of the earliest pieces being the Acorn vase, and you will remember the dog with vase attached number **743/827**, and the lion with spill holder number **819** as mentioned previously in DOGS and OTHER ANIMALS.

Many of the novelty sets such as chimney vase 2425 with an animal, and bulb bowls with rabbits and gnomes had been successfully produced by the time the first more comprehensive SQUIRREL range was put on the market. You can see from the way the numbers are rather spasmodic that first a few pieces were tried, numbers 2457, 2459 and 2468, then gradually numbers 2507, 2512, 2593, 2598, 2600. It seems it was normal to test the market in this way, and wait for reaction to come back from agents as to its success or otherwise, before pressing ahead with more models. SQUIRREL was the first of this type produced by Shaw & Copestake, it had a small squirrel crouching or standing in a recess of the vase or bowl, the vase incorporated the squirrels tail into the design. Where the squirrel is standing it is holding an acorn. Jardiniere number 2598 has one of each type of squirrel. Usually the squirrel is red and the container handpainted with green grass or leaves. It was produced during the 1950s and 1960s.

SEAHORSE was another example of a cautious debut with number 3370, then 3414 and gathering confidence with **3460**, and **3470** to 3475. These usually have seahorse handles, or a seahorse base, which is not the same idea as an entirely separate animal attached independently to a piece as in WOODLAND. I have only seen this in matt colours of either fawn or white, and not in any catalogue or advertisement, except in the brochure on Flower Arranging which has been reproduced elsewhere in this book, which rather leads me to feel it was not widely distributed. It was modelled by Stephan Czarnota and produced during 1963.

WOODLAND, numbers 4231, 4233, 4239 to 4243, and 4287 to 4293, has as its name suggests, a woodland setting. It was originally available in golden peat or peat green, but the peat green was discontinued after a few years. It has various shapes and sizes of vases, posies, pots, bowls and an ashtray. Somewhere at the base of each piece was either a squirrel or a fawn, handpainted in natural colours. It was first produced in 1967/68 and was still in production at the time the factory went into voluntary liquidation in 1982. Collectors may be interested to know that tray number 4288 was re-used and re-numbered **4972** especially for the Galloway Bull Society who commissioned an ashtray with 'Bonnie Galloway' impressed on the base and a Galloway Bull mounted on the ashtray. This has a green base and a black and white bull, obviously only a small number were originally made for the Society.

RIVERSIDE, numbers 4375, 4377, 4385, 4394 to 4395, 4524 and 4547 was also a popular range, in fact my next door neighbour has a piece and she is not even a SylvaC collector. The vase or posies are always green, depicting bullrushes, with a white swan gliding by. It is quite unique and not one I have seen made by any other pottery, whereas you will find several similar designs to WOODLAND made by other manufacturers. Most of it was first produced in 1969 and continued until 1982 except for the floating bowl number 4547 which was discontinued earlier.

HOUSE IN THE GLEN, has a mother rabbit outside a toadstool house and is really cute. It can also be found with a gnome which isn't nearly as nice. Numbers 4789 to 4791 are all vases, and bowl 4886, basket 4887, tray 4888, posies 4889 and 4890. These are not seen very often and either owners like them so much they won't part with them, or it was never very widely produced. I love it, except for number 4889 which is a round rather flat posy, which usually has a gnome or rabbit reclining on it. It is handpainted on either a beige or green background, and was first produced in 1971.

I have reproduced two unique pages from the decorators catalogue showing both RIVERSIDE and HOUSE IN THE GLEN with the original suggested colour schemes hand written in ink.

In 1974 a range of ware with a dolphin strategically placed was produced for a short time, the numbers are 5185 to 5192, the vases and posies themselves were shaped into waves, and coloured blue and matt white, the dolphin was grey and white. This is very pleasing and you will read in the SylvaC Collector's stories how Jane Hallsworth has a soft spot for them, I think she has every piece from the set. It is very cleverly modelled, and there are two sizes of dolphins to match the pieces. One point of interest from the Mould Makers register; written before number 5185 are the words '*Save 12 Nos for Dolphin Range*', in fact only eight numbers were used, the remaining four numbers were eventually taken for other products.

I had thought HIGH TIDE was the same as DOLPHIN minus the Dolphin, but it seems I was wrong. HIGH TIDE numbers are 5481 to 5489, and although the idea of waves is the same as DOLPHIN, they are completely unadorned, and no mention is made of them being connected at all. HIGH TIDE was produced from 1979 to 1982.

In 1975 came the instruction in the Mould Makers register: '*Reserve 12 numbers for field mouse*', and in 1977 ten of these numbers were used for HARVEST TIME. This was delightful, the vases or bowls represented yellow cornfields, and a brown and white field mouse was mounted on the base, except for flower jug 5243 where it was a little way up on a ledge, and basket 5244 where it was on the top. There were two mice the larger number 5251, the smaller 5252, these were modelled by George Matthews and 'ran' from 1977 to 1982.

Towards the end of the life of Shaw & Copestake, in 1981, GIANT PANDA NOVELTIES were produced for a short while. The numbers were 5571 to 5576, 5578 and 5579. This was mostly modelled by George Matthews, and it was available in either amber or green. The vases or bowls represented bamboo trees, and the money box number 5576 resembled bamboo stalks. A little black and white panda was strategically placed on the base of each piece. There were two types of panda, one sitting, number 5578 and one standing, number 5579. Although these little creatures were given mould numbers they are probably too small to actually carry them. This was the last of the novelty vase range to come from the Sylvan Works.

▲ Toadstool number 707 with gnome, pixie, dog and Mother Rabbit. Photograph by Peter Lepino.

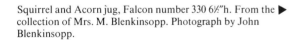 Squirrel and Acorn jug, Falcon number 330 6½"h. From the ▶ collection of Mrs. M. Blenkinsopp. Photograph by John Blenkinsopp.

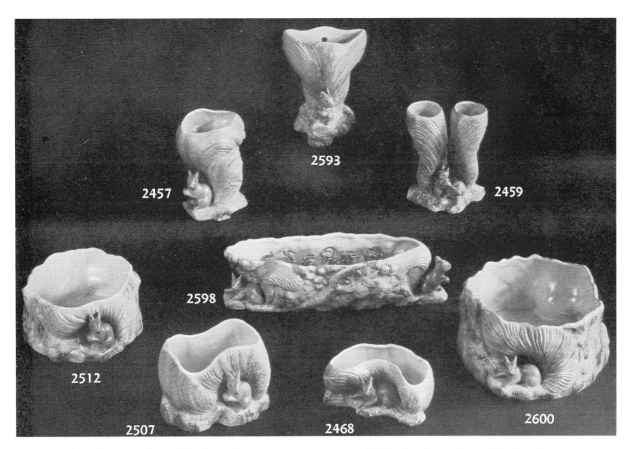

▲ Squirrel range, from a SylvaC catalogue.　　　　　　▼ Woodland range, from a SylvaC catalogue.

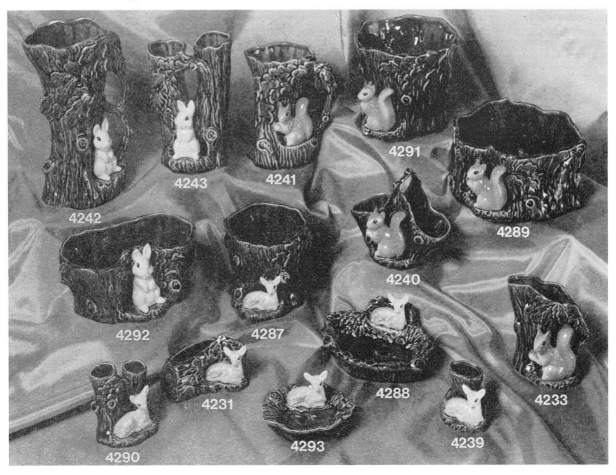

Sylvac

All bases Dip Forest Green GVA 60336
Except l/s bowl 4547 Aero Black inside before dipping

'RIVERSIDE' RANGE

HAND PAINTED SWANS
ON GREEN BASE

4395

4377

4375

4393

4394

4524

4547

4385

Swans Paint- Yellow 1034 Brown 421 Black 1045
Dip Common glaze 2414335

							APPROX. SIZE	
★Vase ...	... 4385	...	...	...	...	...	10·2 cms.	(4″) high
Vase ...	... 4377	...	...	...	...	...	15·3 cms.	(6″) „
Vase ...	... 4375	...	...	...	...	...	20·6 cms.	(8⅛″) „
★Vase ...	... 4393	...	...	...	...	...	8·5 cms.	(3⅜″) „
Bowl ...	... 4394	...	...	...	...	...	19·5 cms.	(7⅝″) long
Floating Bowl	4547	...	...	...	...	...	26·0 cms.	(10¼″) across
★Tray ...	... 4524	...	...	...	...	...	11·5 cms.	(4½″) „
■Candlestick ...	4395	...	...	...	...	...	6·8 cms.	(2¾″) high

★*Sold in minimum quantities of 12.*
■*Sold in minimum quantities of 6.*

▲ Page from the original decorators catalogue with colour instructions c.1972.

SylvaC 'House in the Glen Range'

Colour Selection:— Beige Ground
Green Ground

Handwritten notes (right margin):
Aero Brown
13 R 157
Dip Beige
25 245 171

Aero Black
Dip Forrest
Green
GA 60336

Aero
1pt Penn 1248
1pt orange E 184 X 124
All fittings
dip Common
white

Handwritten notes (left margin):
it ack=
ng

Handwritten note (bottom): Paint Face & ears Brown 1400

Each item is available with either 'Pixie' or 'Rabbit' (except 4889 which has both)

Vase .. 4791	.. 152mm (6") high	Posy .. 4889	.. 210 mm (8¾") across
Vase .. 4790	.. 178 mm (7") ,,	Bowl .. 4886	.. 203 mm (8") long
Vase .. 4789	.. 203 mm (8") ,,	*Tray .. 4888 (min 12)..	115 mm (4½") across
*Posy .. 4890 (min 12)..	120 mm (4¾") long	Basket .. 4887	.. 140 mm (5½") long

All measurements are approximate

Sold only in minimum quantities (colours assorted) where stated

SHAW & COPESTAKE LTD., Sylvan Works, Longton, Stoke-on-Trent, ST3 1PN, England
Telephone: 33037/8 (STD 0782)

▲ Page from the original decorators catalogue with colour instructions c.1972.

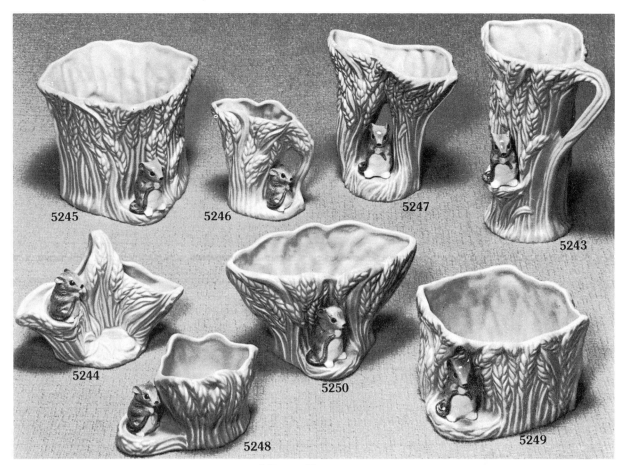

5245 5246 5247 5243

5244 5248 5250 5249

▲ Harvest Time range.

▲ Container number 2829 3¾"h for pens and pencils. One on
the right is from the collection of Darrell Willis-Utting.

Giant Panda Novelties *by* SYLVAC ERAMICS

Nobody will deny that the giant panda is the most popular attraction in zoological gardens throughout the world. With his wistful face, cuddly body and gentle demeanour, he has to be a winner with his innumerable fans.

Choice of Ground Colours: Amber or Green

▲ Page from a SylvaC catalogue.

SylvaC

NOVELTY TANKARDS   HAND PAINTED

				APPROX. CAPACITY	APPROX. SIZE	
Tankard	4570	Skull	... ...	(12 fl. ozs.)	9·8 cms. (4″)	high
Tankard	4574	Drinking Horn	...	(10 fl. ozs.)	14·4 cms. (5⅝″)	,,
Tankard	4584	Riding Boot	...	(10 fl. ozs.)	14·6 cms. (5¾″)	,,
Tankard	4387	Fish	...	(16 fl. ozs.)	15·0 cms. (6″)	,,
★Tankard	4567	Fish	...	(6 fl. ozs.)	11·0 cms. (4⅜″)	,,
★Tankard	4566	Fish	...	(10 fl. ozs.)	13·0 cms. (5⅛″)	,,

★*Not illustrated—shapes as Tankard 4387.*

All items on this page sold in minimum quantities of 3.

▲ Page from an original SylvaC catalogue.

✻ OWL	✻ FROG	✻ CHIPMUNK	✻ BULLDOG	✻ TORTOISE
5106	5097	5105	5096	5101
122mm (4¾") *high*	135mm (5¼") *high*	145mm (5¾") *high*	145mm (5¾") *high*	145mm (5¾") *long*

Caricature Novelty Money Boxes

✻PIG L/S	☐ PIG S/S	✻ TEDDY BEAR	✻ BLOODHOUND
Black	Black	Orange	Golden Peat
3019	1132	5104	5103
190mm (7½") *long*	102mm (4") *long*	133mm (5¼") *high*	133mm (5¼") *high*

✻ ELEPHANT	✻ CHIPMUNK	✻ TORTOISE	✻ OWL
Black	Rockingham	Green	Amber
5102	5105	5101	5106
127mm (5") *long*	145mm (5¾") *high*	145mm (5¾") *long*	122mm (4¾") *high*

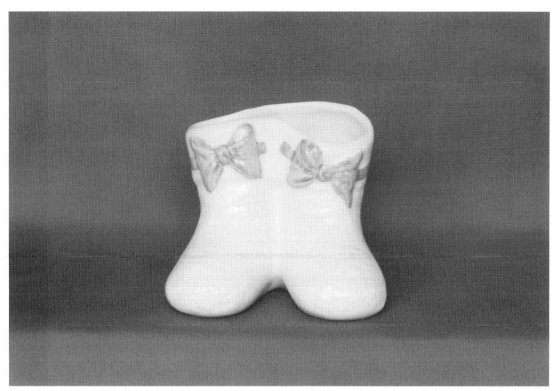

▲ Baby bootees number 5554, available with pink or blue bows.

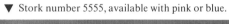

▼ Stork number 5555, available with pink or blue.

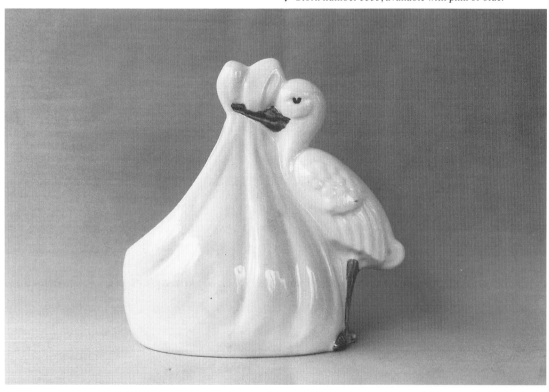

A unique ceramic collection of 'different' subjects based on items which may be found on any desk. These fascinating articles can be adapted or used to suit a whole host of purposes.

Item	Ref. No.	Approx. size mm & in		
'Newspaper' — Holder	5996	116	4⅝	*high*
'Match Box' — Tray	5997	137	5⅜	*long*
'Match Box' — Pen Holder	5998	105	4⅛	*high*
'Sack' — Pen Holder	5999	107	4¼	*,,*
'Scrap Paper' — Tray	6000	133	5¼	*long*
'Gift Parcel' — Box	6001	115	4½	*,,*
'Carrier Bag' — Pen Holder	6002	102	4	*high*
'Parcel' — Money Box	6003	102	4	*long*
'Letter' — Paper Weight	6004	133	5¼	*,,*
'Ball of String' — String Dispenser	6005	92	3⅝	*high*

▲ Page from an original SylvaC catalogue c.1980.

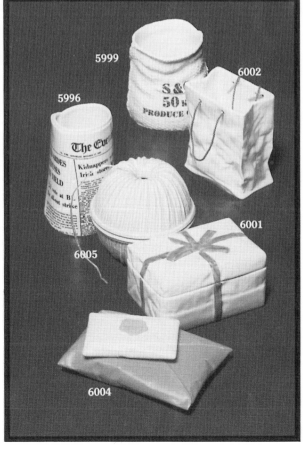

Boxed 'Cottage' Thimble 4831
Thimble 32mm (1¾") *high* Box 63mm (2½") *long*
(Sold only in multiples of 6)

Boxed 'Castle' Thimble 5053
Thimble 32mm (1¼") *high* Box 67mm (2⅝") *high*
(Sold only in multiples of 6)

Boxed 'Windmill' Thimble 5058
Thimble 32mm (1¼") *high*
Box 100mm (4") *high*
(Sold only in multiples of 6)

Boxed 'Leaning Tower of Pisa' Thimble 5057
Thimble 35mm (1⅜") *high*
Box 82mm (3¼") *high*
(Sold only in multiples of 6)

Boxed 'Circus Clown' Thimble 5059
Thimble 32mm (1¼") *high* Box 88mm (3½") *high*
(Sold only in multiples of 6)

Boxed 'Wishing Well' Thimble 5060
Thimble 32mm (1¼") *high* Box 57mm (2¼") *long*
(Sold only in multiples of 6)

▲ Hand painted Novelty Thimbles. Page from a SylvaC catalogue.

GNOMES

Several SylvaC garden gnomes have now been found, and collectors have very kindly sent photographs. They were mostly discovered in small bric-a-brac shops, and all seem in surprisingly good condition considering they had a cellulose finish and were originally meant for the garden. Probably the gnomes which have survived were in fact kept indoors, as there seems to be no sign of weathering on any of the examples I have seen. All are clearly numbered, not necessarily on the base, sometimes the number is found on the side or the back of the item. I was also pleasantly surprised by the amount of detail on the gnomes, the facial expressions and general quality of the modelling.

They are usually very colourfully handpainted in reds, blues and yellows and have smart black footwear. They are numbered as follows: pre-war numbers **962**, **1024**, **1092** to **1095**, **1097**, and 1221, post-war numbers F81 to F83, F87, F108, F110, F113.

Gnomes, Goblins, Gremlins and Pixies etc., seem to be a recurring theme during the life of the Shaw & Copestake factory, the earliest one number **842** having just been found. Lucky Pixies 1420 and 1421, sitting under a toadstool and on a grass mound are frequently seen, and I also have 1421 mounted on ashtray number 1366. They continue to crop up attached to all manner of items, and perhaps some others will eventually be discovered. They are also to be found as part of bulb pots for example number 2339 and wall vases such as number F320.

▲ Garden Gnome number 1092 8¼″h. From the collection of Mr. David Jackman.

▲ Page from a SylvaC catalogue. Low numbers are Falcon numbers.

CHARACTER JUGS

The Neville Chamberlain jug, was a very exciting find for a collector, who also found an advert for it in the Pottery Gazette and Glass Trade Review dated November 1st 1938. The number is 1463, it is hand painted in a matt glaze, 6¼″ high and features a head only.

I have also discovered a character jug of Sam Weller number **1231**, this is a full length character sitting on a chair holding a mug of beer, in hand painted cellulose. The name Sam Weller is very crudely scratched on the front edge of the base, it is 6½″ high. Other collectors have also found a larger Sam Weller number **813** in exactly the same style, 8¾″h. These can also be found in a one colour matt glaze.

There is also a miniature Welsh lady head and shoulders, which is more like a candle holder number 1288 3½″h, and a rather strange little man character jug number **1289** only 2¾″h.

Shaw & Copestake have produced many Character jugs the majority of which were outside modelled by Longton New Art Pottery Co., Ltd., trading under the name of Kelsboro Ware. The moulds were actually used by Kelsboro Ware and you may see some with that mark as well as the SylvaC mark. Later on when the factory was run by Crown Winsor, their logo was used on the bases of the jugs. It is a range that was very popular and continued right up to the closure of Crown Winsor (Pottery) Ltd., in 1989.

Leprechaun 4495　Colonel 4420　Fisherman S/S 4417　Watchman 4452　Churchill 4476
114mm (4½″) High　83mm (3¼″) High　57mm (2¼″) High　50mm (2″) High　108mm (4¼″) High

Falstaff 4479　Mandolin Player 4462　Shylock 4478
152mm (6″) High　203mm (8″) High　165mm (6½″) High

Neptune 4423　Fisherman L/S 4496　Musketeer 4469　Auld Mac 4409
76mm (3″) High　127mm (5″) High　150mm (5⅞″) High　114mm (4½″) High

OLD TOBY (S/S)	OLD TOBY (M/S)	OLD TOBY (L/S)	TOBY (L/S)	TOBY (S/S)	TOBY (M/S)
4406	4405	4404	4401	4403	4402
76mm (3") *high*	102mm (4") *high*	203mm (8") *high*	184mm (7¼") *high*	95mm (3¾") *high*	133mm (5¼") *high*

GAFFER (M/S)	SHAKESPEARE	COACHMAN	SQUIRE
4415	4491	4407	4411
95mm (3¾") *high*	127mm (5") *high*	104mm (5½") *high*	102mm (4") *high*

CAVALIER	HENRY VIII	GRENADIER GUARDSMAN	LIFE GUARD	CHELSEA PENSIONER	YEOMAN OF THE GUARD
4487	4488	4494	4490	4493	4489
115mm (4½") *high*	102mm (4") *high*	127mm (5") *high*	127mm (5") *high*	108mm (4¼") *high*	108mm (4¼") *high*

SAM WELLER	TONY WELLER	MR WINKLE	MR WOLFE (M/S)	MR PICKWICK (L/S)	MR PICKWICK (M/S)
4440	4436	4448	4459	4431	4432
82mm (3¼") high	82mm (3¼") high	83mm (3¼") high	89mm (3½") high	108mm (4¼") high	83mm (3¼") high

ROBIN HOOD	ALLAN A DALE	MAID MARIAN	SHERIFF OF NOTTINGHAM	FRIAR TUCK	LITTLE JOHN
5114	5118	5117	5115	5113	5116
152mm (6") high	160mm (6¼") high	160mm (6¼") high	152mm (6") high	170mm (6¾") high	170mm (6¾") high

GAFFER (S/S)	ANNE HATHAWAY	WELSH LADY	WILLIAM SHAKESPEARE	CABBY	MR PICKWICK (S/S)	MR WOLFE (S/S)	CHARLES
4416	4471	4477	4474	4467	4433	4460	4466
64mm (2½") high	76mm (3") high	76mm (3") high	76mm (3") high	70mm (2¾") high	51mm (2") high	57mm (2¼") high	70mm (2¾") high

PROMOTIONAL AND ADVERTISING WARES

Like most potteries Shaw & Copestake produced a certain amount of promotional, advertising and special orders. One you will probably be familiar with is Tea Caddy number **3372**, with elephant ear handles, known as the Sita Jar. More than one hundred thousand were originally made in 1963 for the well known Rington Tea Company, which is based in Newcastle upon Tyne and covers the area between the Scottish Border and Yorkshire. Each Christmas they offer a promotional pack, usually a pottery item containing half pound of their special tea. SylvaC also made about sixty thousand teapots for them in 1965, they were white with a floral lithograph and gold edge, unfortunately I cannot put a number to this piece.

Many advertising ashtrays were also made but I wonder how many of you have seen one advertising 'Le Moulin de Lecq Inn', which is written around a water-wheel in the centre of the ashtray. The ashtray itself has no number, but is clearly marked with the SylvaC stamp under the glaze. It was first produced in the early 1960s and about three thousand were made over a period of three or four years. Le Moulin de Lecq Inn, was a well known nightspot in Jersey, owned by Mr. & Mrs. Ronnie Ronald, who originally came from the North Staffordshire area. The wheel was a replica of the water-wheel which stood in the centre of the Inn. I have been unable to pin point this Inn exactly, my informant can only remember it was in the centre of Jersey and slightly to the north west.

Ashtray number **5145** was cane coloured and mounted with a Sand Buggy, and number **5146** was charcoal grey with an Aeroplane. They were produced for Lesney Products in 1973. SylvaC made the ashtrays and also mounted them with die cast models supplied by Lesney. These were not advertising wares but meant for re-selling, the project was a failure and only five or six hundred of each was made.

If you have heard of Pipers whisky you will be interested to know of the promotional ashtray and jug SylvaC made in 1978, the jug is number **5435**, and the ashtray **5436**. There was also a Guinness ashtray number **5437**, about three thousand of which were made.

A small order for Ind-Coope in 1981 was a specially commissioned Benskins Indian Head Tankard, only about five hundred were made. The profile of the head stands out from the main body, it is colourfully decorated in red and yellow with the word Benskins in red along the top of the feathered headdress. Benskins was an old established Brewery which was taken over by Ind-Coope, the Red Indian Head was a well known trademark of the company. Although the tankard carries no number I have established that it was in fact **5222**, and modelled by an unknown freelance designer.

There was also a Volvo tankard number 5221, modelled in 1981 by George Matthews. About 100 Ham stands number **5143**, were produced in white, in 1973, I have not been able to obtain further information on these two items.

A number of these orders were obtained through Rodek, which was a small company based in Stone, Staffordshire, who specialised in obtaining merchandise for promotional and advertising purposes. I believe ashtray 5144 was actually used by Rodek themselves, as I seem to remember seeing an ashtray some time ago with the name on it. The company is no longer in business and was disbanded about 1982.

Collectors may be disappointed to hear that the Schweppes Cricketers number 3574 modelled in 1964 by Reginald Thompson did not go into production. It was intended as an advertising line but never went further than the prototypes. Six different models were envisaged, three or four of which may have been made, by which time it was realised it was too costly and complicated a venture and abandoned.

Sometimes an existing mould was re-used for a promotion, such as pot number **4906**, which was previously a holder for a pan scourer or a container for beef or chicken stock. It later re-surfaced as an elegant container for Fortnum & Mason's 'Finest English Blue Stilton Cheese' when the company was under the direction of Longton Ceramics Ltd., and on the base of this pot is the only Longton Ceramics mark I have so far seen.

When Longton Ceramics Ltd., and Crown Winsor took over the Sylvan Works, many commemorative and promotional ceramics were produced using the original SylvaC moulds. The tankards, mugs and ashtrays leant themselves beautifully to different adverts or commemorations. Honey pots were also used for Fortnum & Mason, in shapes of hives and honeycombs. I bought several of these in the Factory Shop before its closure, for just a few pounds. Unfortunately some are not numbered as they were probably modelled after the Sylvan Works was taken over.

Although one thousand Leyland Lorry ashtrays, number 5404, were made in 1977, not many seem to reach the open market. My husband spent many hours on the telephone trying to track one down at the Leyland offices, now Leyland Daf, he was passed from department to department, and given many different phone numbers to try. The result was that one or two were actually found, but the owners could not be persuaded to part with them.

However much more likely to be found is the Harrods van, which was designed and modelled by David Birch of The London Pottery Company Limited, but made in the Sylvan Works by Crown Winsor. It is a beautiful model and was originally on sale in the tea department of Harrods, the roof lifts up to reveal a small packet of tea. Not I suppose strictly speaking SylvaC, but a very collectable piece never the less, and much more obtainable than the Leyland Lorry.

The London Pottery Company Limited, have designed and modelled a number of promotional wares for Harrods and Fortnum & Mason which were made in the Sylvan Works when it was under the direction of Crown Winsor. David Birch is very talented and a former student of the Royal College of Art. He travels all over the world seeking inspiration and specialises in providing containers for the Food Industry. Further details in Appendix C.

Collectors may have noticed an advert in the Sunday Telegraph colour supplement '7 Days' dated November 5–11, 1989, page 25, for a ceramic Christmas tree. This was for '*a limited edition (5000) made in the Crown Winsor Sylvac Works.*' The Christmas tree was in fact a lamp, and one 40 watt bulb lit up many smaller lenses from the inside, it was 15″ high, white or cream and decorated with lace and ribbons. It has no trade mark on the base. Between two and three thousand trees were sold through a distributor Ambrit (UK) Ltd. Shortly after this the Crown Winsor factory went into receivership and the Christmas tree moulds were sold to various potteries in Stoke-on-Trent, and Gloucestershire. They were produced again for the 1990/1991 Christmas season by other manufacturers, in a variety of colours and decorations.

Collectors may also be interested to know that a limited edition of five hundred die cast 1920 model 'T' vans, advertising The SylvaC Story, and made by Lledo London Ltd., for Falkland Promotions, was issued in 1991. It is hoped there will also be a limited edition model specially made to commemorate the publishing of The SylvaC Companion. Further details in Appendix C.

▲ Promotional tankard produced for Benskins Ind Coop in 1981, number 5222 5¾"h. Photograph by Peter Lepino.

▲ The Christmas Tree Lamp, produced by Crown Winsor (Pottery) Ltd., for Christmas 1989 and made in the Sylvan Works. Photograph by Peter Lepino.

◄ This little chap was made in the Sylvan Works in 1989. It is a pie funnel and has no number. Photograph by Peter Lepino.

SYLVAC COLLECTORS

Most SylvaC collectors have an amusing and interesting story to tell about their experiences when collecting SylvaC. I correspond regularly with a number of collectors, and so much enjoy their letters that I asked them to contribute to The SylvaC Companion. They were delighted to do so, and have written amusing anecdotes. They all come from different parts of the country, but share the same enthusiasm for collecting SylvaC.

A COLLECTORS TALE by Norman Hardcastle

While I was looking around an Antique Fair about two years ago, I noticed a green acorn vase with a squirrel handle (number **1115**). Memories came flooding back immediately I saw this, and I conjured up a picture in my mind of Grandmother's sitting room with the squirrel vase on the window-sill. I can remember always being fascinated by it, and wondering who made it. I had forgotten about it until that moment and picked it up to look at and decided to buy it to remind me of my Grandmother, who has long since passed away. It has pride of place on MY window-sill now, with other SylvaC jug/vases alongside it. The second jug I saw was the stork handle one (number **1138**), and then I found the rabbits climbing into the jug (1318), and the gnome and mushroom jug (**1196**). I have even managed to find the birds nest jug (1305) and coconut and monkies jug (**1190**). I have specialised in the matt coloured SylvaC/Falcon Ware jug/vases, but also like any novelty or interesting shaped jug. I find the concept of using creatures in place of handles extraordinary.

On one stall at a Bric-a-brac and collectables market I saw two identical Dorothy Bag jugs, number **F406**. One was half the price of the other, and when I looked at the cheaper one, could see no obvious damage to account for this. However the dealer explained why; apparently the cheaper one was marked Falcon Ware and therefore was a forgery, whilst the SylvaC one was the genuine article. I decided to buy the 'forgery', much to her surprise, but she had to admit that it was a good copy!

I also collect the miniatures to go with the larger jugs, and have a nice collection of those too. As my house was built in the 1930s I have tried to keep to the pre-war styles to fit in with the atmosphere, although there is bound to be some creeping in of the later pieces, but I try not to go beyond the 1940s SylvaC if possible. I also admit to a passion for the flying duck wall plaques, and have tried to collect these in matt glazes, which has proved very difficult. At the moment I have various colours and sizes, which look quite effective.

I suppose my reason for collecting SylvaC is to bring back my childhood memories of the 1930s and 1940s, pure nostalgia really. I find it an enjoyable hobby and most weekends are now taken up with the search for additional pieces. I cannot afford to be fanatical about it, and have to choose my pieces and count my pennies very carefully. Quite a number have been bought very cheaply at Boot Fairs and Bric-a-brac markets and I am sure they are a good investment. I live near the Twickenham Rugby Ground, and there is sometimes a very large boot fair there which I have found worth visiting.

I was quite surprised to realise that other people also collect SylvaC, I had somehow thought I was the only one. But it appears there are now thousands of us, so it is just as well there is plenty of it to go round, although I have noticed it has become more scarce lately.

I have also noticed when watching the television quite a few pieces of SylvaC appearing as part of the set decor, and I was watching the film 84, Charing Cross Road, when I spotted a Sylvac/Falcon ware jug on a sideboard. Quite a few magazines also use SylvaC props now as well to decorate their photographs.

Perhaps it is becoming more acceptable at last and will no longer be considered the Cinderella of Collectables.

MY SYLVAC MEMOIRS by Jane R. Hallsworth

How did it all start? For me, it was on a Sunday morning at a local fleamarket in Trowell Parish Hall near Ilkeston, Derbyshire. Graham, my husband, and I decided to browse around on the spur of the moment. Inside there were only ten or twelve stalls, mostly local people selling unwanted bits and pieces. You know the kind of things; books, toys, various bric-a-brac, clothes, shoes and kitchen ware. On one stall a woman was selling a variety of pottery items and amongst them was our very first piece of SylvaC. It was number 2276 pixie on an oval flower holder, at a cost of £2.75. We got talking to the trader and we were informed that SylvaC was beginning to become popular to collect. How prophetic of her!

During our first year of collecting we spent many wonderful week-ends searching for pieces of SylvaC, travelling near and far, always expressing delight when our quest brought to light another piece for our collection. We hadn't any information about SylvaC to help us, so we had no idea as to what was or was not SylaC. We picked up many pieces that weren't and it is now obvious we must have missed pieces that were. To collectors who are just starting, Susan's book The SylvaC Story is without doubt a must and will help them seek out that elusive piece at Antique and Collectors fairs. I know how much hard work Susan put into her book and I feel honoured to know her and to call her my friend.

Lots of information came from the traders we met and we have made many new friends over the five years we have been collecting. One of my favourite pieces was from a special lady trader who has become a very dear friend to us both. The piece we bought from her was number **3927**, a fox feeding a chicken with corn. Hidden behind his back he holds an axe, the expression on his face is devilishly one of hunger.

Our collection has steadily grown and we have many pieces now. Buying has slackened off considerably to how it was when we first began collecting, and we are trying to collect sets rather than a piece of everything. We get a great sense of achievement when we are finally able to buy a particular item we have been searching for, especially when it is at last put on our shelves, even more so when it completes a set. It is a most rewarding and fulfilling hobby. Once you are bitten by the collecting bug you are beyond all medical help!

We have specialised in collecting dogs, character jugs and wall plaques, with a large overall smattering of everything else, like bunnies, vases, cats, various animals and of course not forgetting the elves and pixies. I am also particularly fond of the Dolphin Range as each piece is set with waves and a dolphin. For me it is a lovely way to have a reminder of the sea in your home.

I call to mind a strange bit of good fortune that you often get when collecting. We were told there was a set of three SylvaC hats, I bet you know the ones I mean, number F733 boater, number F732 trilby and number F721 flat cap. Well, within the space of only four weeks we acquired all three at different fairs. The boater in green we got at Chilwell Olympia Sports Centre, the trilby in fawn from Loughborough Town Hall and the flat cap in fawn all the way from Bingley Hall in Stafford. Until those four weeks we had not seen them before and we've not seen them since. It never fails to surprise me! We've found its often the way, many items of SylvaC seem to appear all around at the same time, or equally as mysteriously disappear. Its either a lot about or nowt!

We once found out about character jugs after we had been to a fair in Ilkeston, I remember it was near Christmas, my favourite time of the year. We'd been looking at some SylvaC dogs on a traders stall, when the trader pointed out to us that she had a set of four in the Robin Hood character jugs. Until that moment we didn't even know they made such things. We bought all four pieces, they were number 5114 Robin Hood, number 5116 Little

John, number 5117 Maid Marion and number 5118 Allan-a-Dale. We were convinced there must be a Friar Tuck, and set out looking for him. A few months later at Newark, we came across number 5115 the Sheriff of Nottingham, the dealer we bought him from informed us there was indeed a Friar Tuck, number 5113, and we had just missed buying him that day. It took us two more years of searching, then at a fair at Castle Donnington Exhibition Centre, joy oh joy, we found Friar Tuck to complete the set. You must never give up hope on that elusive piece, also having the patience of a saint does help.

One weekend we went to an Antique and Collectors fair in Hucknall Leisure Centre, and on this occasion we had already spent a lot of money on SylvaC and were actually on our way out and back to our car when we saw a rather nice vase incorporating a seahorse, on a shelf on a stall by the door. We were both delighted to find it was SylvaC number **3460** in fawn. The dealer was asking £6.50 for it, not a princely sum of money you may think, but I tell you we had to search our purses, pockets and linings to come up with it, and we only managed to scrape together £6.00. What a nail biter, would he let us have it cheaper, thankfully he said he'd take our £6.00. The moral of this story is always take your cheque book and card, I want no more irregular heart beats thank you very much!

I rather enjoy watching the expressions on peoples faces when they walk into our home for the first time, and see our collection. Some are truly amazed, some just gape and stare, some say 'Oh Jane, I'm glad I don't have to clean it all'. Others say nothing, just stand looking at it, and I've even had the odd one who was totally oblivious to it and made no comment at all. Its very interesting watching the different affect it has on people, seeing their varying expressions can be most amusing.

I have a feeling of contentment when I'm in my favourite armchair, slowly surveying our collection of SylvaC, and when my eyes rest on certain pieces, memories come flooding back of places and lovely people we've been able to meet. Its a good feeling inside and for me especially its what collecting is all about. Don't you agree?

▲ The author (on the right) visiting her friend and fellow collector Mrs. Jane Hallsworth in 1990. Photograph by Peter Lepino.

MY SYLVAC STORY by Jenny Hulme

It all began with one small blue bunny given to me by my mother-in-law who purchased it from a local jumble sale for ten pence. It looked lovely on the shelf by my new baby's cot. On my travels I noticed a green one. How nice, they can keep each other company! Then there was the dark blue one, little did I realise the forces moving over me. Of course, it was too late, I was totally hooked and the search was on to find the matching pink, fawn and yellow ones.

Very soon, although I had other things to buy I began to scour the stalls, primarily for SylvaC. Eventually my highly trained eye could spot almost every piece in the room within minutes.

My in-laws being retired could attend many more fairs than myself and began to produce a constant stream of rabbits crawling up the handles of jugs, kissing on a match-holder and perching on ashtrays. I made a decision to concentrate on the blunt-nosed bunny and the quest was in full swing at the beginning of 1982.

At one antique fair I gaped in horror at I watched a rare yellow rabbit No. 3097 change hands twice. I finally found the last dealer in the chain and implored her to consider selling it to me when she had sorted out a price. Half an hour later she came over to me and said in deadly earnest 'I'm afraid its just got to be eight pounds'. I gave her ten. She was pleased, but that was nothing to the sheer pleasure of actually owning my first satin-glossed yellow rabbit.

Once, after a very exhausting school trip on a hot summer's day, the coach pulled up at some traffic lights and just as we were pulling away, I saw the familiar, sleek outlines of a green sausage dog No. 2595. As soon as the coach reached school, I was straight down the corridor and on the phone. I had managed to remember the name of the shop, (with the help of 74 excited children). The telephone number was in the directory. 'Hello! . . . Yes? . . . You've still got it? . . . How much? . . . Five pounds? . . . Is it damaged?', 'A little' came the reply. More like a lot, I thought. 'Hold it for me.' So they did. Minor damage to the foot . . . super on the shelf.

In the search for SylvaC every source was fully explored. The Laura Ashley Home Decorating Book showed a mucky, purple bunny. Surely not SylvaC? . . . It wasn't long before two of them both bearing the SylvaC stamp were cluttering up yet another corner of the room.

It wasn't until Susan's first book that I realised how important it was to collect only recognisable SylvaC, that is with a stamp or number. Out of my collection of three hundred bunnies over a hundred were mongrel, so out they went. However there are a number of instances where the glaze was so thick that it obscured the markings altogether, except for the odd number or letter.

Since I live in the centre of the Potteries in Stoke-on-Trent, my enthusiasm to learn about SylvaC has given me a much deeper appreciation of pottery making and pottery people. After the launch of Susan's book I was amazed to find that I knew a few people who had worked at the SylvaC factory. Some of the last items to come out of the factory before it closed were not to my liking, but I suppose in time they will become collectable.

The set of pink-mottled ducks, which can be found quacking in order of size across most furniture showroom sideboards were purchased upon the strict instructions of my nine year old son. As was the 'Deco' lamp (a pair of hands holding a spherical glass shade) exclusive to Argos. One spectacular piece is the Christmas Tree made at the SylvaC factory in 1989. It has pride of place amongst my collection along with my two rarer pieces, a blue Jemima Puddleduck (Mrs. Duck) No. **1157**, and a green Pigeon No. **1377**. Nowadays, I just collect blue, pink and yellow pieces which seem to be much rarer.

Although confined to one room, my collection is, as all collections should be, an immeasurable source of pleasure to me . . . and finally, who said you can't pick up a SylvaC bunny for 50p anymore? My headmistress did exactly that at the Church Bazaar the other week. Of course, she gave it to me . . . well naturally, they don't call me the 'Bunny-Girl' for nothing!

COLLECTING SYLVAC by Timothy Mark

I didn't intend to collect SylvaC, in fact I only went out for a loaf of bread, down to the corner shop. Having bought the bread I casually glanced into our local antique shop, situated next door, where I buy the odd objet d'art and work of art. Sitting incongruously on a Queen Anne china cabinet was a ghastly green dog. Our eyes met and for some unearthly reason I found myself drawn into the shop. The owner, Jack knows me quite well, and followed my gaze to the Queen Anne cabinet. 'A very fine piece Tim' he said, 'look lovely in your dining room'. 'Actually I was looking at the green dog,' I said. 'What can you tell me about it'. Jack looked at me askance, after all I was previously known as a chap with infinitely good taste. 'Nothing to tell' said he, 'an old lady brought it in, and feeling sorry for her I gave her a couple of quid for it, as you know Tim I don't normally deal in such trivia. Its just a cheap piece of mass produced pottery, probably 1930s'. The wretched dog was still looking at me, 'I'll give you a fiver for it', I said.

Jack looked at the dog with renewed interest, it was a large Scottie about 12″ high in deep green. He tried to find some redeeming feature to comment on, but seemed lost for words, and feeling rather embarrased at my obvious lack of taste I hurried from the shop.

I excitedly unwrapped my purchase at home with a feeling of real decadence. 'Whats that' said my wife, 'A dog' I said, 'I can see that' she said sarcastically, 'why have you bought it'? I was really on the defensive here, and was asking myself the same question. 'Well . . . its a typically 1930s piece of Art Deco pottery' I said lamely, 'you can see how well modelled it is, its very well defined, the colour is unusual I agree, but surely you can see its attraction, its the sort of thing thats going to become very collectable in a few years'. I was clutching at straws here, but to my surprise my wife said 'Yes I can see it does have some merit, but it doesn't exactly fit into our decor, still we can perch it on top of the kitchen dresser'.

A few weeks later I had a call from Jack, the old lady had been in the shop again selling some more green dogs, was I interested? I tried not to sound too excited, and said I would pop in if I was passing, which I happened to be that afternoon. Three more green Scottie dogs, graduating in size stared at me once again from the same cabinet. Well it seemed a pity to separate the set, so yes they are now all looking at us from the top of the kitchen dresser.

So this sparked my interest in green pottery animals, and if Jack came across any, he always let me know. One dog, a terrier with a sideways glance, had a name on the base, SylvaC, this inspired me to look in The Goddens Directory, and was the first clue I had about the maker of these matt green animals. Not that it helped much, as no one had heard of them and they appeared not to exist any more. We started to be regular attenders at all the local Antiques Fairs and Markets, looking for anything green then moving on to fawn coloured animals. By this time my wife was as keen as I was and nearly had heart failure when she spotted the figure of a lady, in a beautiful shade of green. Could it be SylvaC, it looked right, the numbers were done in a similar way to our other purchases, it was £28.00 so we took a chance and bought it. We were very anxious to know what other output was available from this factory.

We travelled to a larger Fair one Sunday, and saw a gent who had quite a large selection of SylvaC for sale, seeing my interest he asked if I was a collector. I reluctantly admitted I was, and he asked if I had the book on SylvaC. Now this was just the breakthrough I was looking for, I eventually tracked it down, and read it from front to back, from back to front, and inside out. I was delighted to find the green lady was shown in one of the photographs, but found that several of my green animals were 'foreigners', so they were quickly discarded. I have to admit I did panic a bit when I saw the vast array of animals I still had to collect, and each trip out became more and more vital.

I also tracked down the author of the book, and Susan now receives desperate phonecalls from me as to whether £100 is a good price for this or that. She always tells me to calm down, and wait until next week when I will see the same item at half the price, and of course I usually do. Or sometimes I see something of doubtful origins and try to pick her brains, she usually tells me to buy it anyway if I like it, it may turn out to be rare S & C, if not, does it matter?

I have managed to discipline myself to only collect the animals, apart from the green lady, and they do look rather good on our kitchen dresser, now taking up nearly all the shelves. I was very chuffed to see in an issue of the magazine called 'Hello!' an 'at home' article on the musician and composer Chris De Burgh. A photograph taken in his rather grand Castle shows an identical 'Mac' Scottie dog which first sparked my interest in SylvaC.

We decided to decorate our sitting room recently and were packing up all the ornaments, amongst which was a very ornate Victorian vase all gilt and handpainted with colourful lanterns, which we had bought many years ago. As I started to wrap it up I happened to notice that on the base was a Daisy. Yes, believe it or not, sitting on our mantlepiece for the last 20 years has been an old Shaw & Copestake vase.

These last few years collecting SylvaC animals have been most enjoyable. Tramping around the Fairs is great fun, and I am pleased my first instinct to buy 'Big Mac' was a sound one after all!

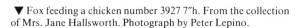
▼ Fox feeding a chicken number 3927 7″h. From the collection of Mrs. Jane Hallsworth. Photograph by Peter Lepino.

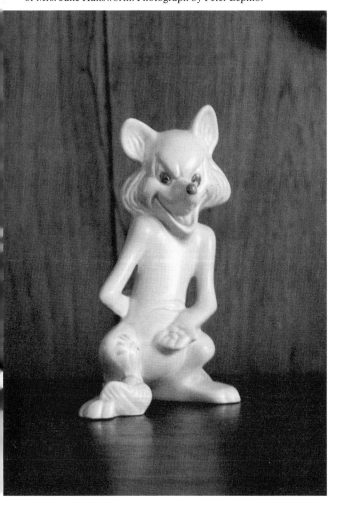

▲ Tray with fox and chicken egg cups number 4546 5½″h. From the collection of and photograph by Mrs. Jane Hallsworth.

FALCON WARE – PRODUCTS OF THE FALCON WORKS

Produced by Thomas Lawrence (Longton) Ltd.,
            Falcon Works
            Waterloo Street,
            Longton,
            Stoke-on-Trent.

These notes explore the range of wares and patterns being manufactured by the factory from 1888 until 1938, when it came under the directorship of Mr. Richard Hull of Shaw & Copestake Ltd. After 1938 the output has been well documented, and although they had an independent range of Falcon Ware items also used some SylvaC moulds.

The address of the factory is given as Falcon Works, or Falcon Pottery. Sometimes a Falcon bird is used as the trade mark. Unfortunately much of the early ware was not marked, but incised or embossed range names were sometimes given to pieces. With the help of other collectors I have been able to list some of these, together with some gold decoration numbers and descriptions of lithographs.

Some of the pieces were marked with L and G, (standing for Lawrence and Grundy) above a scroll with the words 'Falcon Ware'. The mark of an urn was also used with T. Lawrence above it, and Falcon Ware underneath, and Falcon Ware on an artists palette was sometimes used. Photographs of the various trade marks are shown on pages 69 and 70 of The SylvaC Story. A recently discovered mark has been one of a laurel wreath surrounding the Falcon Ware name, I cannot be sure this is a Thomas Lawrence mark, but other collectors seem to think it is.

It is important not to confuse these marks with the J.H. Weatherby & Sons (Ltd) Falcon Ware. Their factory in Hanley, Stoke-on-Trent was also called Falcon Pottery, and the name Falcon Ware was often incorporated into their trade marks. Usually it also has J.H.W. & Sons in the mark, further information about these can be obtained from the Encyclopaedia of British Pottery and Porcelain Marks, by Geoffrey A. Godden, F.R.S.A.

The Thomas Lawrence (Longton) Ltd., factory was founded in 1888 by Mr. Thomas Lawrence, it was originally in Wharf Street, Stoke-on-Trent, and moved to Falcon Works, Waterloo Street, Longton in 1898. The factory still stands and is now used by the John Beswick Company, which is now part of the Royal Doulton Group. From about 1920 the Managing Director of the factory was Mr. Lawrence's nephew Mr. John Grundy. Mr. Grundy's daughter eventually married Mr. Richard Hull junior, Managing Director of Shaw & Copestake Ltd. Due to the sudden demise of Mr. John Grundy in 1938 three days after the business was made a limited company, Mr. Richard Hull and Mr. E.J. Dennis gallantly stepped in and took over the directorships.

Although I have found no documented literature about the factory apart from a few references in The Pottery Gazette, I did see some interesting scrapbooks while being taken on a guided tour of the Sylvan Works, in 1989. While our guide was showing us the amazing contents of many of the nooks and crannies of the factory I spotted an old book full of Thomas Lawrence's decoration samples. From what I remember, these were cut out and glued into a large book, with handwritten comments and numbers alongside. Some had come from other countries such as Germany. I thought this to be of great importance and suggested my guide take great care of it, which hopefully he has.

No doubt the Sylvan Works held many such secrets about Shaw & Copestake and Thomas Lawrence, the difficulty is making people understand the significance of it all. When I originally approached the factory management for archival information in 1986 I was catagorically assured there were no documents or anything of any historical interest on the site. This proved to be quite untrue as I was later to discover, but I was never able to take advantage of any of my findings as the Receiver took over the factory before I could return and document or photograph these items of such importance.

In the early days of the factory Mr. Thomas Lawrence tended to specialise in producing vases, flowerpots, jugs, toiletware, and ten and seven piece trinket sets. He was described as 'a manufacturer of quick selling lines in decorated earthenware at moderate prices'. Another of his specialities was a range of childrens toy trinket sets and toiletware. On these sets 'some very attractive controlled and copyright patterns' were used. (Pottery Gazette 1928).

Later on, in the late 1920s and 1930s the range was extended and highly decorated tableware and ornamental items were produced, amongst them biscuit barrels and sandwich sets. The influence of Mr. John Grundy can be clearly seen in the artistic nature of the decoration, and a signed handpainted vase dated 1897 is still in the possession of his daughter Mrs. Eileen Hull. Although he was managing director of the company, he was usually to be found in the decorating shop of the Falcon Works, experimenting with ideas for decorating designs. He was also a very talented artist, and his daughter Mrs. Eileen Hull, still has many of his paintings. He probably hand painted many of the vases himself, and was fascinated with the idea of projecting photographs on to vases.

Although much of the early ware is hand painted or of a printed and filled in design, by the late 1920s the lithograph method was being used which was sometimes extended by the decorators to give it greater life and character.

When looking for Falcon Ware pieces, one is immediately drawn by the fine quality of some of the wares, and the striking patterns and decorations. Most of the decorations were numbered and some are described at the back of this book. Unfortunately the Falcon Works did not use mould numbers until about 1940, when they started at No. 1 using them consecutively. Although quite a number of the pieces had range names, it has not been possible to make a very full list to date. Some of the pieces were marked Falcon Ware, but many pieces were not marked in any way.

Another problem has been the way other pottery manufacturers were using the same design of lithographs, which one sees repeated on different ranges. The Crinoline Lady with the hollyhocks being a good example, Falcon Ware produced a lovely toilet set with this design, yet I have a cake plate made by Kirklands, Embassy Ware, with an almost identical design, and it was a favourite of a manufacturer using the trade name Empire Ware. One collector has a lovely Falcon Ware sandwich set which is complete with six plates in mint condition, all decorated with the Crinoline Lady.

One of the best selling decorations was the Flight of Swallows, which was used for many years on toilet sets, flowerpots, vases, jugs and fancies. A very similar design called Lovebirds was also used by Shaw & Copestake, and can be found on their vases, and toiletware.

Although only two examples of Falcon Ware clock sets have so far been seen, one of which was marked ESSEX and Falcon Ware, I am sure a few others were designed. A former employee at the Thomas Lawrence Falcon Works remembers seeing clock sets in the warehouse, which seems to indicate they are authentic Thomas Lawrence products.

Also found by a collector has been a magnificent Toucon on a tree stump, it is marked Grecian which is the decoration design and colour. I presume it was made for use with a floating bowl as there are holes in the stump for inserting flowerstems. It has not been possible to date this, and we are looking for other examples of this type, no animals or figures from this era have come to light so far. It was not until Mr. Richard Hull took over the factory in 1938 that there was a abundance of animals and a few figures, which were mostly designed by Mr. Reginald Thompson B.E.M.

Mr. Thompson was the longest serving employee of the factory, starting at the Falcon Works in 1917 at the age of 14, and finishing as Chief Designer of the Shaw & Copestake Sylvan Works. He retired at the age of 75 in 1978, having been the youngest decorating manager in the Potteries at the age of 19. His daughter Jeanette has inherited some of his finer pieces of work, a few of which have actually been signed by him.

Just before World War II Falcon Works made a special order of pottery pigs for a butchers shop, these were very large about 14" long, judging by the photographs. Perhaps because of the outbreak of the war, the pigs were never collected by the customer and lay in the warehouse for many years. There was quite a celebration when they were eventually sold to a client after the war, which warranted a photograph in The Bulletin (the Staff Magazine). They were probably bought for a butcher's window display, but despite searching many shops I have not been able to locate one.

It has not been possible with the limited paperwork available to date any of the early Falcon Ware pieces, other than to judge by the style of design and decoration. Going back to the example of the Crinoline Lady, this was a popular 1930s design. An earlier example of a 1920s style would be the Morocco Border much loved by all decorators and the public for quite a few years. A similar pattern was also used by Shaw & Copestake and many other manufacturers.

Not many adverts appeared in the Pottery Gazette for the Thomas Lawrence wares, but I have reproduced an example from the 1928 edition. The other photographs have come from collectors of early Falcon Ware.

Thomas Lawrence (Longton) Ltd., Falcon Works, produced their own lines quite independently of Shaw & Copestake, until they moved into the new combined factory in 1957. Items were marked either Falcon Ware or SylvaC, some even had both marks. The SylvaC flying duck wall plaques numbers 1360, 1401 to 1403, and several other ranges, were made at the Falcon Works, which was probably a result of the two factories using the same premises, (the Falcon Works) during World War II, when some of the moulds were obviously left behind.

Thomas Lawrence (Longton) Ltd., ceased trading in 1962 when no more items using the Falcon Ware name were produced, and the company was finally wound up in 1964.

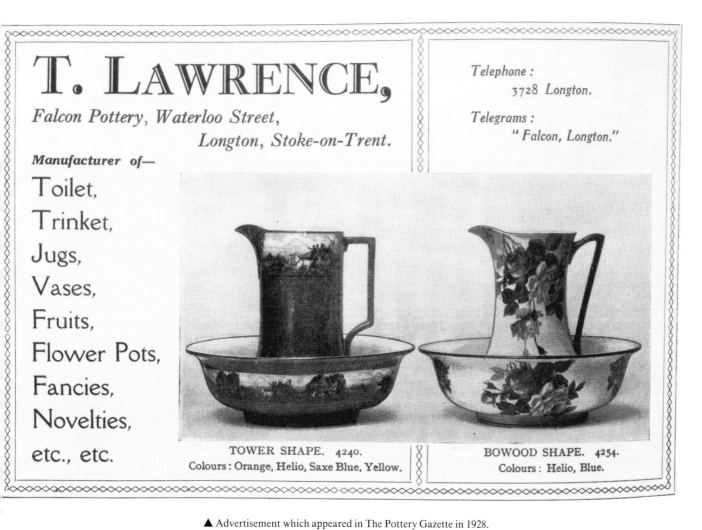

Advertisement which appeared in The Pottery Gazette in 1928.

▲ This photograph accompanied an article about Thomas Lawrence in The Pottery Gazette in 1928, and shows decoration number 4298.

▼ Staff group from Thomas Lawrence (Longton) Ltd., c.1947, with the large Falcon Ware pigs. In the centre of the front row is Mrs. Harriet Ainsworth, who was in charge of the Finished Warehouse at the Sylvan Works until 1942, then at the SylvaC section in the Falcon Works until 1947, completing 50 years service. Photograph kindly lent by Mrs. Helen Evans nee Stewart who is on the left in the front row.

▲ Televisions were presented to staff completing more than 25 years employment. From the left in this photograph are Mr. & Mrs. Richard Hull, Mr. Reginald Thompson, Mrs. M. Alcock, Mr. E.J. Dennis, Mr. Jim Brian, Mr. Jim Betts, Mr. Gater, Miss D.E. Ridgeway. Mr. Dennis is presenting Mr. Betts with a retirement cheque. The photograph was taken in the Falcon Works canteen c.1949, and kindly lent by Mrs. Helen Evans nee Stewart.

▼ Three Falcon Ware novelty jugs. Duck number 43, Dog number 45 and Rabbit number 44. They are all marked Falcon Ware. Photograph by Peter Lepino.

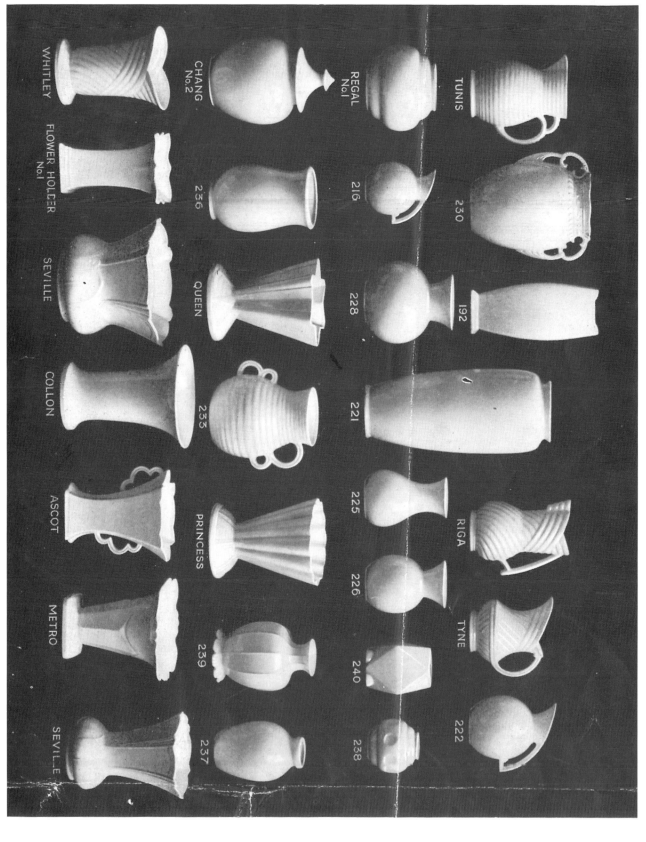

'FALCON' WARE SHAPES

THOS. LAWRENCE (LONGTON) LTD., FALCON WORKS, LONGTON, STOKE-ON-TRENT.

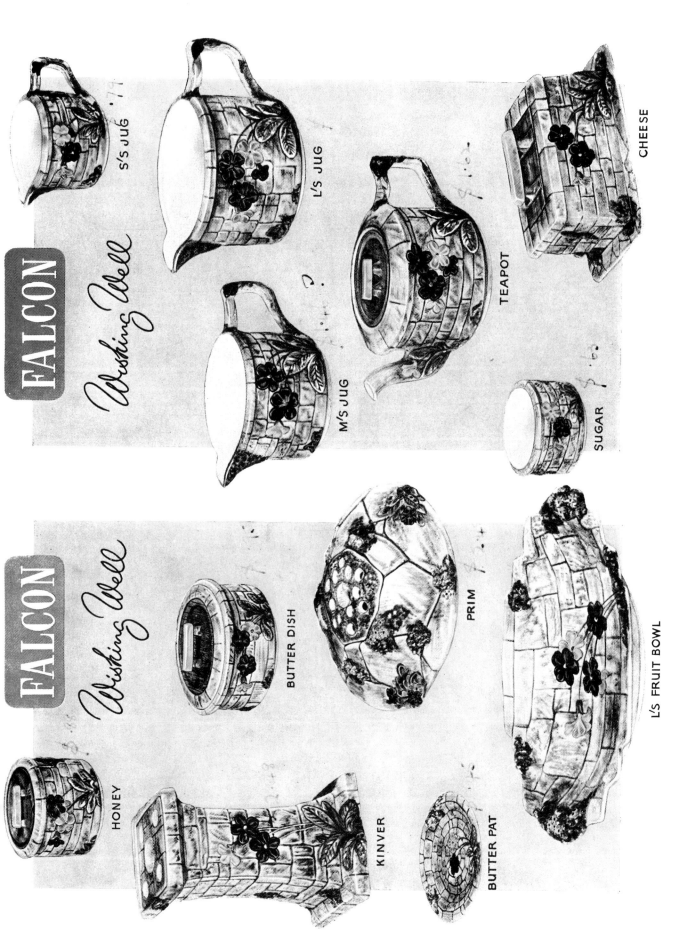

▲ Falcon Ware Wishing Well range. From a Falcon catalogue with hand written amounts in dollars for the export market.

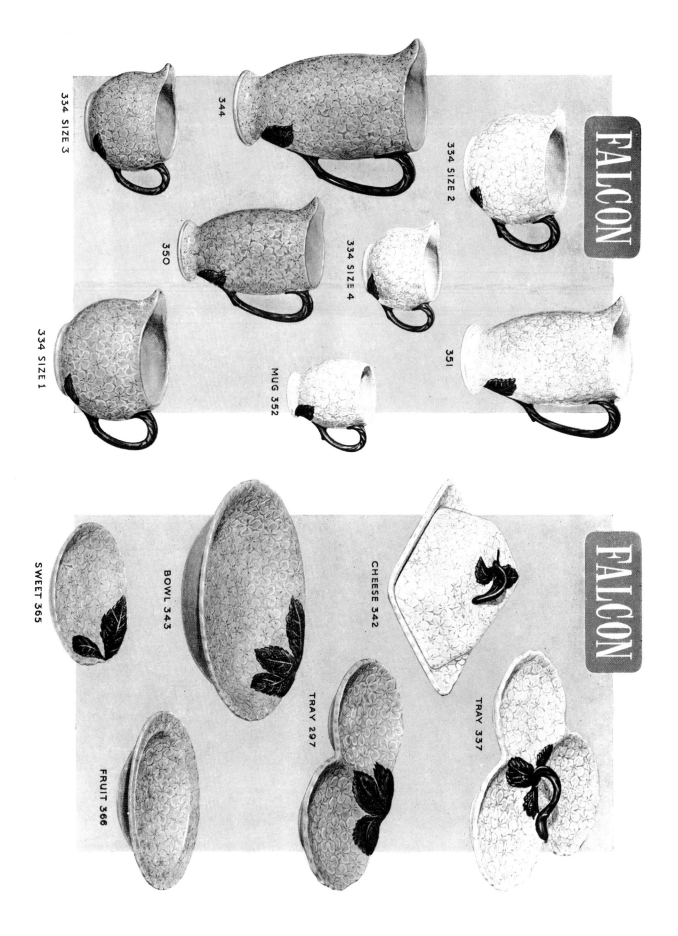

FALCON

334 SIZE 3

344

334 SIZE 2

350

334 SIZE 4

334 SIZE 1

351

MUG 352

FALCON

SWEET 365

BOWL 343

CHEESE 342

FRUIT 366

TRAY 297

TRAY 337

▲ Falcon Ware Hydrangea range which was available in pink and primrose with green handles and leaves. Page from a Falcon catalogue.

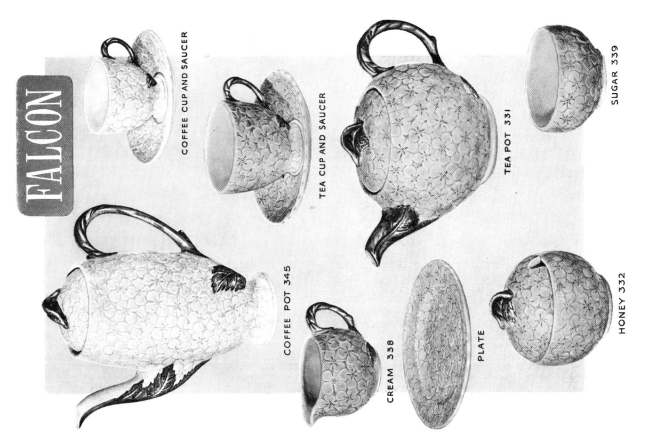

▲ Page from a Falcon Ware catalogue.

Falcon

*Posie Bars
and Bowls*

BURLEE No.3 M101 6"

BURLEE No.2 M101 Asst. 8"

BURLEE No.1 M101 Asst. 8"Dia.

418

1113

368

BOWLS

Burlee Posies

CAN ALSO BE
SUPPLIED IN PLAIN
COLOUR GLAZES

▲ Page from a Falcon Ware catalogue with hand written amounts in dollars for the export market.

Sydney

WALL VASE 524/MATT

Flowers

Page Nineteen

BOWL 479/MATT

FRUIT BOWL 500/MATT

BOWL 479/MATT GREEN ARRANGED WITH FLOWERS

JUG 490/MATT

JUG 501/MATT

Australian

▲ Page from a Falcon Ware catalogue.

VASE 221

BOWL 252

$ 3.51

VASE 380

Rosslyn

FRUIT BOWL HUDSON

$ 5.35 CRESCENT BASKET

VASE 196

JUG
Made in 3 Sizes
272 12"
259 10"
260 8"

Page Seven

▲ Page from a Falcon Ware catalogue, showing hand written prices in dollars for the export market.

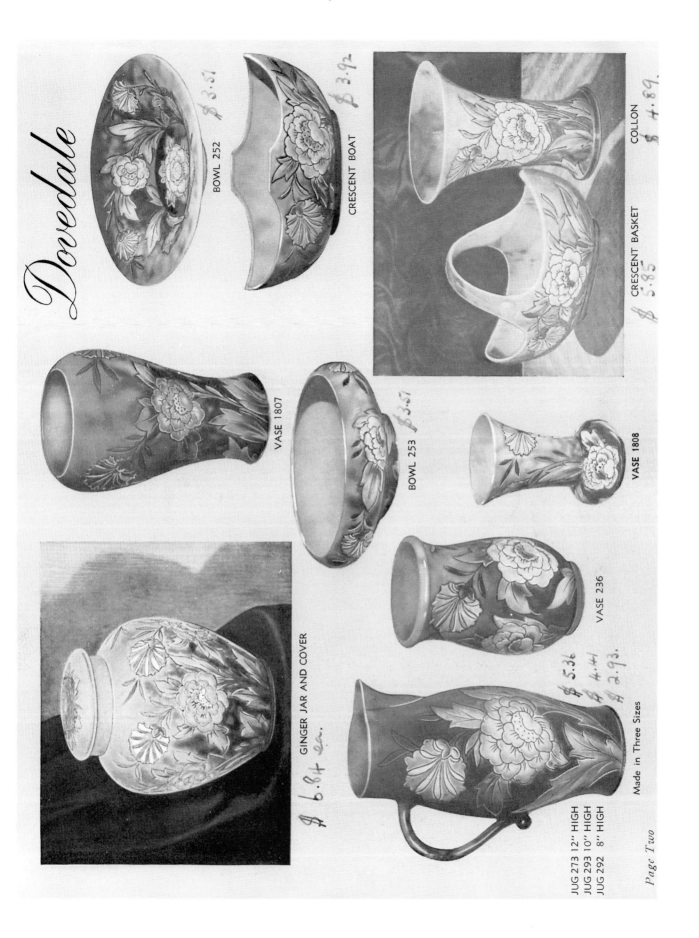

Dovedale

BOWL 252 $ 3.51

CRESCENT BOAT $ 3.92

COLLON $ 4.89.

CRESCENT BASKET $ 5.85

VASE 1807

BOWL 253 $ 3.51

VASE 1808

VASE 236

GINGER JAR AND COVER $ 6.84 ea.

$ 5.36
$ 4.44
$ 2.93.

JUG 273 12″ HIGH
JUG 293 10″ HIGH
JUG 292 8″ HIGH

Made in Three Sizes

Page Two

▲ Page from a Falcon Ware catalogue.

145

Falcon "Argosy"

Argosy Pattern has White Matt Ground with Coloured Ship decoration. See pages 8 and 9 for shapes on which it can be supplied

▲ Page from a Falcon Ware catalogue.

FALCON

Sonora

226

218

376

399

246

▲ From a Falcon Ware catalogue.

SylvaC

CUCUMBER
DISH 536

JUG 455

T.V. SET

CHEESE DISH 530

LETTUCE DISH

SALAD BOWL

TOMATO PLATE

▲ Dovecote range. Falcon Ware numbers.

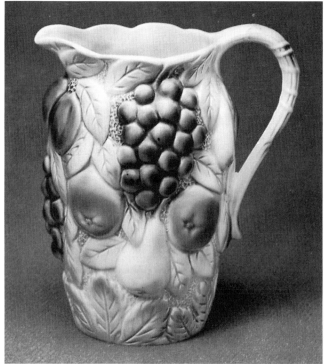

◀ Vine range jug, Falcon number 465 8″h, hand decorated.

FALCON WARE SHAPE OR RANGE NAMES

These names are incised/impressed or embossed on the base of Falcon Ware pieces. Several different shapes have been found with the same name indicating the name refers to a range of wares rather than individual shapes. Where only one piece has been found with a particular name, this has been described, but does not necessarily mean it is the only item with that name.

BOWOOD	Range of toiletware. Pottery Gazette 1928.
BUNGALOW	Range of toiletware.
CAIRO	Jug.
CASKET	Rosebowl.
CHATSWORTH	Range of toiletware. Hexagonal shape.
CRESCENT	Basket with handle. Pottery Gazette 1942.
CUBAN No. 2	Jug. Squarish.
EMPRESS	Vase. Round. Pottery Gazette 1942.
EMPIRE	Biscuit Barrel. Round.
ESSEX	Vase, part of clock set. Eiffel Tower shape. Inside the base of the clock which a collector has is inscribed: To Minnie, from Lily and Florrie. Xmas 1931.
HADDON	Biscuit Barrel. Octagonal.
HADDON No. 2	Vase. Octagonal.
HENLEY	Vase with two asymmetrical handles. Pottery Gazette 1942.
MASONA No. 2	Rosebowl.
METRO	Flower holder with ceramic holder in top. Square base opening out to trumpet shape, scalloped rim. Pottery Gazette 1942.
RUTLAND	Range of toiletware.
SEVILLE	Flower holder with ceramic holder in top. Round base, narrow waist opening out to scalloped rim. Pottery Gazette 1942.
SEVILLE COMBINATION	Hexagonal vase with ceramic holder in top, 7½″ high. Pottery Gazette 1942.
SIAM	Jug, centre narrowing. Pottery Gazette 1942.
STANDARD	Butter or cheese dish. Round 3″h 4″diameter.
TOWER	Range of toiletware. Tall well-balanced shape. Pottery Gazette 1928.
TULIP	Oriental style vase with two handles and an incised border.
VICTOR	Range of toiletware.
UNIVERSAL No. 3	Jug. Round.

Numbers after the names probably indicate sizes of vases or jugs in that series.

▲ Falcon mark of the 1920s and 1930s.

▲ Falcon mark of the 1940s.

▲ Falcon mark of the 1930s and 1940s.

FALCON WARE DECORATION NUMBERS

Decoration numbers are usually handpainted in gold on the base of the item. Information has been obtained from the Pottery Gazette and Glass Trade Review, and collectors of Falcon Ware.

4240   Old time coaching scenes, applied in the form of a wide border at the top of a coloured ground. Colours: orange, helio, saxe blue, yellow. From Pottery Gazette 1928.

4254   All over style depicting a cluster of roses. Colours: helio and blue. This is a very lively type of treatment, the design being not merely transferred, but 'extended' and picked-in with colour, so as to give it greater life and character. From Pottery Gazette 1928.

4291   Powerful floral style of decoration in the form of a broad ribbon and rose. From Pottery Gazette 1928.

4298   'Derby' colourings of a rose with lattice effect. This pattern might well be mistaken for a printed and filled in design whereas it is really a lithograph, capable of being produced at a very modest cost. From Pottery Gazette 1928.

4315   An Eastern subject aptly named the 'Morocco Border'. From The Pottery Gazette 1928.

4396   A highly colourful arabian street scene, with a desert background.

4435   Willow pattern with a blue and gold border.

4453   Japanese lady, similar to 4706 but with the addition of a pagoda, and boats.

4621   An Arab sitting on a camel.

4706   Japanese lady standing with a parasol, looking at a Japanese plant. On the reverse of the design is a lantern decorated with bird. Similar to 4453.

4745   Crinoline lady with hollyhocks.

4792   Ornate floral design, with gold decoration.

4912   Glorious Devon. Thatched cottages surrounded by hollyhocks, two figures in the distance.

4961   This number is on a very colourful Indian Chief bookend.

4988   Lady wearing pink dress sitting under a May blossom tree in a pretty garden. This was also used by Shaw & Copestake.

4991   Cottage, water, water lilies, flamingo, flowers.

5063   Homestead.

5138   Fireside Tavern.

5146   Ye olde flower shop, with crinoline lady in doorway.

5160   Coach and four driving out of the archway of an Hostelry. Reverse side has a sign post for Exeter.

5173   Incised pattern of trees and flowers, very colourful.

▲ Falcon mark c.1940s.

Recently discovered mark, thought to be from the Thomas ▶ Lawrence factory, probably pre-war.

FALCON WARE DECORATIONS WITHOUT NUMBERS

These decorations have been found on Falcon Ware pieces by the author or other collectors, or, where there is no description, have been mentioned in The Pottery Gazette and Glass Trade Review. They are printed on the base or written in the corner of the decoration.

Village Smithy	A country cottage. Pottery Gazette 1941.
Copse	Tree and flower decoration. Pottery Gazette 1941.
Dove Cote	Pottery Gazette 1941.
Down Somerset Way	Colourful street scene. This lithograph was also used by other manufacturers.
Flight of Swallows	For an inexpensive pattern, this is very lively in its colouring and yields the maximum of effect, although its means of execution is simple. Pottery Gazette 1928.
Grecian	Orange/yellow/blue colours blended together.
Lahore	Large daisy type flowers. Pottery Gazette 1942.
Midsummer Day	Pottery Gazette 1941.
Rose and Crown	Coaching scene. Pottery Gazette 1941.
Spinning Wheel	Pottery Gazette 1941.
Starglint Ware	White and gold stars on a red background. Pottery Gazette 1956.
The Dell	Colourful flowers and grasses.
The London Road	Crinoline lady emerging from a coach and four.
Tralee	Flowers. Pottery Gazette 1942.
Gretna Green	Marriage by special licence.

▲Country Scenes, a range of Falcon Ware.

FALCON/SYLVAC MOULD NUMBERS
for the 1940s and 1950s

THESE NUMBERS WERE GIVEN TO WARES MADE IN THE THOMAS LAWRENCE FACTORY, DURING THE 1940s AND 1950s, AND MOSTLY PRODUCED DURING THOSE TIMES. IF AN END OF PRODUCTION DATE IS KNOWN IT IS ENTERED AT THE END OF THE COLUMN. ITEMS MADE IN THIS FACTORY MAY BE MARKED FALCON WARE OR SYLVAC WARE. THE FOLLOWING INFORMATION IS NEW, CORRECTED OR ADDITIONAL TO THAT FOUND IN THE SYLVAC STORY. Many of these numbers have come from collectors, the star * after the number means it has not been confirmed.

43	Duck	Jug	4¾"h	
52 *	Ducks	Two joined together	3½"h	
68	Elephant	Standing	9"h	until 1982
130	Penguin	Standing upright with head to right	6¼"h	
131	Penguin	Stooping with head to right	4½"h	
134	Bear	Sitting upright	5½"h	
196	Jar	Ginger jar with cover		
		Misty Morn range	9½"h	until 1982
197	Jar	Ginger jar with cover		
		Misty Morn range	10¾"h	until 1982
216	Jug	Round body, shaped top angular handle	5½"h	
223	Vase	Misty Morn range	7½"h	until 1982
226	Vase	Sanora & Misty Morn range		
		As 228 smaller	6½"h	until 1970
228	Vase	As 226 larger		
233	Vase	With decorative asymmetrical handles	M/S	
237	Vase	Oval, plain, narrow top	M/S	
238	Vase	Round with round indentations	S/S	
239	Vase	Oval, fancy base, narrow top, ridged	M/S	
240	Vase	Diamond pattern, with feet	S/S	
262	Tray	Springbok ware		
266	Honeypot	Springbok ware		
267	Cream Jug	Springbok ware		
268	Sugar Bowl	Springbok ware		
275	Vase	Springbok ware		
276	Vase	Springbok ware		
277	Bowl	Springbok ware		

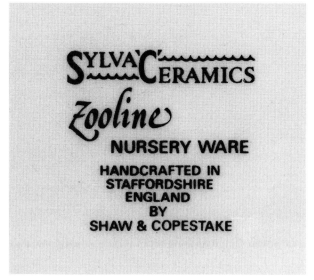

▲ SylvaC mark found on baby plate showing the rarely seen Shaw & Copestake.

▲ A rarely seen Longton Ceramics Ltd mark used by them c.1983.

280	Hat	Flower holder, cream with blue or cream ribbon	6"dia	until 1960s
321	Wall vase	Scalloped edges	8¼"h	
330	Jug	Acorn with squirrel handle	6½"h	
336	Jug	Swallows	10"h	
347 *	Vase			
359	Dish	Fruit, two handles, brown/red matt finish		
369	Pot	Fern, embossed with leaves, assorted colours	7"h	until 1982
381	Wall vase	As a ribbon	5"dia	
384	Holder	Galleon		
400	Jug	Miniature jug vase	3"h	until 1982
406	Jug	Dorothy bag, assorted colours, matt	7"h	until 1982
410	Pot	Assorted colours, three sizes, one is	4½"h	
413	Bowl	Fruit. Vine range HP	12¼"h	until 1982
414	Basket	Vine range HP	10"l	until 1982
419	Pot	Flower. Assorted colours	4"h	
452	Posy	Curved	7"l	
465	Jug	Vine range HP	8"h	until 1982
475	Vase	Miniature jug vase with stork handle	3"h	until 1982
478	Jug	Vine range HP	6"h	until 1982
513	Jardiniere	Shell range	4½"h	until 1975
514	Jardiniere	Shell range	6¼"h	until 1975
538 *	Bear	With trousers, braces, scarf		
539 *	Squirrel	With acorn	4¼"h	
546	Jardiniere	With budgie or flowers, also black with white flowers	6½"h	until 1965
582	Honey	As orange with green lid	3½"h	until 1982
583	Honey	As Pineapple with green lid	3½"h	until 1982
585	Honey	As Strawberry with green lid	3½"h	until 1982
623	Vase	With handles	7"h	
625	Vase	'Fish' shaped	7¼"h	
626	Vase	Cone shape fluted with embossed circles around base	7¼"h	
628	Vase	Classic range, white matt	8"h	until 1982
688	Vase	Treetrunk with blue tit	7"h	until 1982
689	Jardiniere	Treetrunk with blue tit	11"h	until 1982
730	Vase	Pineapple shape	10"h	

▲ An original pre-War Wild Duck label, used on that range.
Kindly lent by Jayne L'Epine-Smith.

▲ SylvaC mark used in the 1960s.

SHAW & COPESTAKE and SYLVAC MOULD NUMBERS

The following numbers are a few of the many issued by the Shaw & Copestake factory. Assuming they were issued chronologically from about 1900 one can roughly date the original mould number. This of course does not allow for re-using the mould at a later date and although the earliest number I have traced is 127, there were probably lower numbers, and wares without numbers before that.

The Registered Design Numbers are a good guide to dating wares, and I have given these where possible. The Registered Numbers are design or pattern numbers that were registered at the Patent Office, High Holborn, London, and it is possible to date these with a li issued by that office.

The following numbers have been found since the publication of The SylvaC Story which incorporates the main body of numbers, an is new or corrected information. In the book 'Shaw & Copestake, the Collectors Guide to early SylvaC', the author has specialised researching the early period and has more complete and detailed information of those numbers. Where the production dates or end c production dates are known this has been inserted in the end column. A star * indicates the source has not been confirmed.

127	Pot	For fern or large plant, round, wavy top turned over slightly	7"h 9"dia
185	Jardiniere		
251 *	Bowl	Similar in style to 436	9¼"dia
255	Vase		
262	Pot	For plant	
273	Vase	With handles	9"h
279	Vase		
281	Vase	With handles. Highly ornate	
302	Jardiniere		
310	Vase		
321	Vase		
335	Vase	With handles. Highly ornate	10"h
337	Vase	With handles. Highly ornate	12"h
338	Vase		
347	Vase	Two handles each side	
362	Pot	For plant	
365	Vase		
371	Vase	With handles. Highly ornate	10"h
374	Vase	With handles. Very ornate	11¼"h
375	Vase	Tall, fluted, on feet, with handles	
376	Jardiniere	With handles on four feet	
387	Vase	With angular handles	11½"h
399	Pot	Embossed shells, decorated with boats. Fluted edge to rim	4½"h 4½"dia
416	Vase		
418	Vase		
419	Vase	With handles. Tall and thin	11½"h
420	Vase		
421	Vase	Oval with narrow neck	7½"h
422	Vase	Square base, oval body, narrow neck	8½"h
425	Vase	With handles. Shorter version of number 419	9"h
426	Vase		
432	Vase	Highly ornate	7¼"h
433	Clock	Small for bedroom	5"h
433	Vase	For spills to match above clock	4"h
436	Bowl	Also used with 700 Kingfisher	9½"dia until 1960s
439	Vase	Narrow neck. Four sided	
445	Vase		
446	Vase		
484	Shaving Mug	Traditional design. The example seen was bright orange with a black and orange chequered pattern round the rim	3¾"h
489	Bowl		
492	Rose Bowl	With grid.	
495	Vase	Hexagonal. Angular handles	11½"h
496	Vase	With handles	
509	Vase	With handles. Very ornate	10"h
510	Clock	Very ornate. Large size	
511	Vase	To match above clock	
521	Vase	Almost straight. With handles	12"h
523	Tray	For dressing table	13½"l
538	Vase		
539	Vase		
540	Vase	With handles Same design as 562	8"h

41	Vase			
48	Vase	Hexagonal. Angular handles		
59	Bowl	For roses with gold mesh top	5½″h 7″dia	
60	Jug	Hexagonal		
62	Vase	Very grand. With handles	14″h	
63	Jug			
65	Vase	With handles		
67	Vase	With handles. Very ornate	11½″h	
70	Vase			
73	Jugs	Straight various sizes	5¼″, 6″, 6¾″ & 7¼″h	
75	Rose Bowl	On plinth. With handles	8½″h	
		Gold coloured mesh top to hold roses		
76	Vase	Square base. With handles	11″h	
78	Vase	With handles	6¾″h	
80	Pot	For plant. Very ornate. Four fluted feet	4″h	
82	Vase			
83 *	Vase	Very ornate. With handles		
85	Vase			
87	Vase			
94	Tray			
00	Vase	With handles as 610 & 611	9¼″h	
03	Pot	For plant		
04	Clock	Ornate with pillars	12″h	
05	Clock	With handles	9¼″h	
06	Vase	To match above clock	7¼″h	
08	Clock	Clock similar to 605	11½″h	
09	Vase	To match above clock	9½″h	
10	Vase	With handles matches 600 & 611	7½″h	
11	Vase	With handles matches 600 & 610	11⅝″h	
13	Vase			
14	Vase	Hexagonal with a narrow neck	9¾″h	
22	Vase	Oval shaped with narrow neck	14″h	
34	Vase	For spills	6″h	
35	Vase	For spills, with real silver rim	4–5″h	
36	Vase			
40	Tray			
43	Cheese Dish	Oblong		
48 *	Vase	To go with 649 clock old style		
49 *	Clock	Old style quite different to shape of 649 below	11½″h	
49	Clock	With handles. Wild Duck range		
		also plain	10″h	
50	Vase	To match above clocks	7½″h	
51	Clock			
54	Plate	Sandwich set comprising six round plates and		
		narrow sandwich plate		
59 *	Vase			
66	Jug	Octagonal	14″h	
75	Plate	For wall		
78 *	Vase			
79	Vase	With Arabs		
93	Jardiniere	Embossed garden scene with couple		
94 *	Tray	For dressing table set	13¾l x 6¼″w	
96	Clock	Three piece set		
00	Bird	Kingfisher to go with floating bowl number 726		
		and later 436	6½″h	until 1965
03	Vase	Embossed garden scene as 693 & 704		
04	Pot	Embossed garden scene as 726, 703	4¾″h	
11	Bowl	Shallow embossed flowers	2½″h 11½″w	
22	Bowl			
26	Bowl	For Kingfisher number 700	9½″dia	
43	Dog	Airdale terrier, with vase number 827 attached.		
		Cellulose finish	7″h 9″l	
44	Clock	With handles	Large	
68	Elephant	Standing	4″h	until 1982
69	Elephant	Standing	6″h	until 1982
70	Elephant	Standing	7¼″h	until 1982
71	Elephant	Standing	8½″h	until 1982
72 *	Camel	With howdah	7″h 9″l	
73	Elephant	Standing. With howdah	8½″h	

776	Pot	Basket weave design, with embossed flowers.		
		Cellulose finish	6"h	
780	Vase	Bulbous base narrowing to centre	5"h	
784	Vase	Wild Duck range	7½"h	
785	Vase	Wild Duck range	5¼"h	
787	Flying Duck	Flower stand		
788	Elephant	With howdah	6"h	
789	Elephant	With howdah	7"h	
795	Bird	Swan		
798	Elephant	With howdah		
801	Vase	Wild Duck range. Reg. No. 768695 (1931/1932)	10"h	
803	Candlestick	Wild Duck range. Reg. No. 769028 (1931/1932)	4"h ?	
804	Trinket Box	Wild Duck range. Diamond shaped.		
	with Lid	Reg. No. 769029 (1931/1932)	3"h	
809	Jardiniere	Wild Duck range. Reg. No. 769285 (1931/1932)	9½"l 5½"h	
813	Jug	Character. Sam Weller as number 1231	8¾"h	
814	Elephant	With howdah	5¼"l 4"h	
815	Elephant	Standing	4½"h	until 1982
818	Lion	Standing		
819	Lion	Standing with vase or spill holder attached.		
		Quite large.		
822	Plinth	For lion		
825	Plinth	For lion		
826	Elephant	With howdah	4½"h	
827	Vase	Attached to dog number 743	4¾"h	
828	Vase	Ribbed, two handles, shape of Greek Urn. Black matt		
829	Jug	Egyptian design	7¾"h	
831 *	Clock	Egyptian design. Goes with vase 832		
832	Vase	Egyptian design. Possibly part of clock set.		
		Reg. No. 774557 (1932/33). Shape: Round with a		
		column each side. Very colourful	7½"h	
833	Vase	Egyptian design. Cellulose finish		
		Reg. No. 774557 (1932/33)		
835 *	Bowl	Egyptian design		
837	Rose Bowl	Egyptian design. Should have flower grid	4¾"h 6"dia	
838	Vase	Egyptian design. Cellulose finish		
		Reg. No 774557 (1932/33)		
839	Vase	Egyptian design. Cellulose finish. With narrow neck	7½"h	
840 *	Urn	Egyptian design. Two handles		
841 *	Bowl	Egyptian design		
842	Goblin/Genie	Sitting on mound	5½"h	
843	Cat	Sitting. With wing collar and bow tie	8½"h	
848	Vase	Oval poppy		
849	Dish	For cheese. From Southsea in gold	5¾"l	
861	Vase	Semi Porc.		
862 *	Clock			
880 *	Vase			
881	Figure	Spanish dancing lady	9½"h	
882 *	Vase			
883 *	Vase			
884	Vase			
891	Dutch	Clog		
898	Jardiniere	Diamond shape	10"l x 5¼"h	until 1970s
903	Ginger Jar	Embossed poppies with lid	12"h	
907	Vase			
917	Pot	For plant. Embossed carnations.		
		Cellulose finish	app. 7"h	
919	Figure	Dancing lady	8½"h	
920	Figure	Dancing lady	8½"h	
926	Pot			
931	Figure	Pierrot	8¾"h	
935	Jug			
944	Vase	Cone shape. Embossed Arabian scene	6"h	
945	Pot	With lid. Embossed Arabian scene. Colourful		
		cellulose painting. Arab sitting on lid	5¼"h 5½"dia	
954	Jug	For cream		
955	Bowl	For sugar		
956	Jug	For cream		
961	Shoe	Also with flowers	5"l	until 1960s

962	Gnome	For garden	5″h	until 1950s
964	Jug	Embossed carnations	7½″h	
974	Jardiniere	Embossed carnations		
987	Vase	Carnations	11″h	
990	Bunny	Round. Assorted colours	5″h	until 1975
992	Shoe	Puss in shoe	5″l 4″h	until 1940s
999	Several collectors have written in with the information that this is a jug, but it seems it is actually number 666!			
001	Flower Jug	Cellulose decoration of orange and blue flowers	7″h	
002	Vase	On foot. Flared top	11″h	
008	Vase			
011	Vase	Shaped with narrow neck	8¾″h	
014	Vase	Bulbous base narrowing at neck. Base green and blue. Top decorated with flowers. Silver coloured rim	8½″h	
022	Figure	Black boy with banjo	5″h	
024	Gnome	Sitting	4½″h	
026	Bunny	Round. Assorted colours	7½″h	until 1970s
027	Bunny	Round. Assorted colours	8½″h	until 1940s
028	Bunny	Round. Assorted colours	10″h	until 1975
032 *		Possibly egg cups and stand		
033	Figure	Red Indian Chief, sitting	7¼″h	
038 *	Dog	With bow round neck	3″h	
039	Vase	Kingfisher		
043	Dog			
044	Dog	Bulldog, with bow round neck	8½″h	
046	Cat	Frightened cat. Assorted colours. As 1313	6″h	until 1960
061	Vase			
064	Bunny	Round with holder, striker or posy	4″h	until 1956
065	Bunny	Round. Assorted colours	6″h	until 1975
066	Rabbit			
067	Bunny	Round. Assorted colours	4″h	until 1975
070	Flower Jug	With handle. Ribbed	11″h	
075	Vase	With embossed flowers		
078	Jug			
086	Cat	Usually black. Sitting	5¼″h	until 1989
087	Cat	Usually black. Sitting	7″h	until 1989
088	Cat	Usually black. Sitting	9″h	until 1940s
090	Mug	Cider mug. To match 1091 ribbed	3½″h	
091	Jug	Cider mug. To match 1090 ribbed	8″h	
092	Gnome	For garden. Standing	8¼″h	until 1940s
093	Gnome	For garden. Standing	9½″h	until 1940s
094	Gnome	For garden. Standing	14″h	until 1940s
095	Gnome	For garden. With pot	8¼″h	until 1940s
097	Gnome	For garden. With pot	9½″h	until 1940s
099	Cat	and Basket		
109	Vase	Art Deco style – matches 1384 wall vase	7″h	
112	Vase			
113	Bowl	Embossed with figures	10½″l 5¾″h	
114	Vase	Embossed with hollyhocks	7¾″h	
115	Vase	Acorn with squirrel handle	8½″h	until 1950s
116	Jug	With dragon handle	8½″h	
117	Dog	Sitting. Large head, mongrel	7″h	
118	Dog	Sitting. 'Monty' the mongrel	6″h	
119	Dog	Sitting. With bow. 'Daisy' dog	4″h	until 1956
120	Dog	Mongrel. Sitting	3¾″h	
121	Dog	Terrier. Standing	4½″h	until 1956
122	Dog	Sealyham. Standing	3½″h	until 1956
123	Dog	Standing	3½″h	until 1940s
125	Vase	Bacchanti range		
127	Swan	Posy holder	5½″l	until 1982
132	Pig	Money-box	4″l	until 1982
134	Jug	With shamrock pattern. (Witch pot)	2½″h	
135	Pot	Witch pot. See 4187 in TSS	3¾″h	until 1940s
136	Bowl			
138	Vase	With stork handle. No snip	10″h	until 1950s
140	Bowl	For sugar to match 1134	2½″h	
142	Squirrel	Sitting	5½″h	
143	Squirrel	Sitting	7″h	
144	Squirrel	Sitting	7¾″h	until 1940s

1145	Squirrel	Sitting	8½"h	until 1940s
1146	Squirrel	Sitting	9½"h	
1147	Jug	Squat. Art Deco. Green/Orange	6"h	
1148	Vase	Shaped like a light bulb, two solid handles at top	8¾"h	
1149	Vase	Cellulose and other decorations	7½"h	until 1960
1150	Flower Jug	Round, ribbed	5¼"h	
1154	Boy	Whistling		
1157	Duck	Mrs. Duck	8"h	
1158	Duck	Mr. Duck	9"h	
1159 *	Cat	With corkscrew tail	6¼"h	
1161	Girl	Shy		
1162	Cat	With corkscrew tail. Reg. No. 806569 (1935/36)	3¾"h	
1163	Cat	With corkscrew tail	7¼"h	
1164	Cat	With corkscrew tail	11"h 8"l	
1167	Vase	Hunting with stag heads handle	L/S	
1168	Dish	Oval	11½" x 7½" x 2"h	
1170	Girl	Black. With banjo? To match 1022	5"h	until 1940s
1173	Vase	Ribbed with two asymmetrical knobs	7"h	
1174	Jug	For flowers. Triangular shape	10"h	
1175	Jug	Pilgrim shape (description from catalogue)	6¼"h	until 1960s
1176	Vase	Ribbed	7¼"h	
1177	Vase	Ribbed	8¼"h	
1178	Flower Pot	Ribbed	7¾"dia	
1181	Ashtray	With hare & striker number 1270, probably with other additions	2½"h	
1182	Rabbit	As used on 1312	2½"h	
1183	Cruet	With stand. Seen P.G. 1937	5"dia 2½"h	
1184	Honey	Seen P.G. 1937		
1186	Posy Bowl	Number given in catalogue but no description	8"dia	
1187	Spill Vase	Number given in catalogue but no description	4¼"h	
1189	Flower Jug	Triangular shape	11¼"h	
1190	Vase	Two monkeys climbing into a coconut. Reg. No. 809067 (1936)	7"h	until 1940s
1191	Dog	Begging. Joey on collar	5"h	until 1965
1192	Dog	Begging. Joey on collar	6"h	
1193	Dog	Begging. Joey on collar	8"h	
1194	Dog	Begging. Joey on collar	9½"h	
1195	Vase	Acorn with squirrel handle	7½"h	until 1950
1196	Vase	Mushroom. Two gnomes for handle. Reg. No. 809115 (1936)	8½"h	until 1950
1201	Vase	Bulb shape	5"h	
1203	Dog	Alsatian, sitting, matt	9"h	
1210	Jardiniere		7¼"h	
1213	Butter Dish	Round ribbed		
1214	Flower Pot	Ribbed	7"dia	
1215	Flower Pot	Ribbed	8¾"dia	
1218 *	Dutch Clog	Plain	7"l	
1231	Character Jug	Sam Weller	6½"h	
1235	Flower Holder	Diamond shaped ribbed as two 1324s put together	10"l 2"h	
1238	Elephant	Standing on one leg, dressed in football shorts and jumper	8"h	
1249	Posy Bowl	Like an upsidedown hat	6"dia	
1252	Flower Jug		6"h	
1253	Flower Jug		6"h	
1254	Flower Jug		6"h	
1255	Rabbit	Table mat holder (originally with mats)		
1257	Flower Holder	Round	7¾"h	
1267	Flower Pot	Ribbed	8"dia	
1268	Flower Pot	Ribbed	9"dia	
1269	Flower Pot	Ribbed	10"dia	
1272	Vase	Fan shape with handles, matches number 1275 (Shell design)	7¼"h	
1275	Vase	Matches 1272 (Shell design)	6"h	
1276	Flower Jug	Shell design	6"h	
1277	Flower Jug	Shell design	7"h	
1278	Fruit Bowl	Shell design	11"dia	
1280	Vase	Shell design	8½"h	
1281	Flower Jug	As 1277	9¾"h	
1284	Lamb	Standing. As 1285	4"h	1930s–1968

1285	Lamb	Standing. As 1284	5″h	
1286	Cat	Sitting, mouth open. Bow around neck	4″h	
1289	Jug	Miniature character	2¾″h	
1290	Penguin	Standing	4″h	
1292	Hen Ashtray	Tail Matchholder	4¼″h	until 1940s
1293	Duck	With body as ashtray	3½″h	until 1940s
1294	Bunny	With body as ashtray	5½″l	until 1940s
1295	Dog	Griffon, sitting	5″l	until 1956
1313	Cat	Frightened Cat as 1046	L/s	
1314	Posy	Plain, or Art Deco type green, yellow, brown triangular shapes	3¾″h	until 1960s
1324	Posy	Boomerang shape	11″l	1930s
1363	Jug	Spiral design	7¾″h	
1364	Mug	Spiral design	3¼″h	
1368	Butter Dish	Spiral design		
1369	Dog	Sitting, Alsatian puppy	5″h	until 1940s
1377	Bird	Pigeon	4″h	
1384	Wall Vase	Art Deco design, matches number 1109 vase	7¼″h 8¼″w	
1414	Dog	Sitting	5″h	until 1970
1415	Dog	Skye Terrier standing	5″h	until 1970
1436	Mug	For cider, Barrel range	3½″h	until 1940s
1438	Dish	Round, Barrel range	until 1940s	
1456	Mug	Barrel range. Similar to 1436 slightly different handle	3½″h	
1463	Jug	Character. Neville Chamberlain	6¼″h	until 1940s
1464	Tortoise	One piece	3¼″l 2½″h	until 1940s
1475	Dog	Sitting, with right paw raised, matt colours	7¾″h	
1476	Dog	Sitting, with right paw raised, matt colours	11″h	
1482	Candlestick			
1571	Vase	Various colours	10″h	1940s–1970
1646	Dog	Playing, partner to 1647	3″h	1940s
1647	Dog	Eyes shut, partner to 1646	3½″h	1940s
1653	Bowl	Embossed flowers. Could be Dahlia range	5¼″h 9½″l	1940s–1960s
655	Jug/Vase	Embossed with flowers	8¼″h	during 1940s
678	Duck	Ski-ing	2″h	during 1940s
679	Duck	Ski-ing	2¾″h	during 1940s
680	Duck	Ski-ing	5¼″h	during 1940s
696	Bowl	Sugar/honey. Handles. Leaves	4″h	during 1940s
719	Vase	Embossed leaves	5½″h	during 1940s
728	Jug	Barrel range	3¼″h	during 1940s
747	Cheese Dish	Neptune ware. Blue body and white handle		during 1940s
748	Tray	Neptune ware. Blue body and white handle	11¼″l	during 1940s
765	Bowl	Sugar to go with Dogs Head range		
781	Vase	Embossed flowers, straight sides, could be Dahlia range	6½″h	during 1940s
794	Jug	Squashed look	4½″h	1940s–1960s
797	Tray small	Neptune ware. Blue body and white handle	S/s	during 1940s
798	Tray twin	Neptune ware. Blue body and white handle		during 1940s
812	Teapot	Neptune ware. Blue body. Seahorse		during 1940s
813	Sugar bowl	Neptune ware. Blue body. Two handles. Seahorse		during 1940s
814	Cream Jug	Neptune ware. Blue body. Seahorse		during 1940s
815	Jug	Neptune ware. Blue body. Seahorse	Three sizes	during 1940s
820	Box	Trinkets, hand painted flowers on lid, assorted colours	3¼″h	1940s–1960s
822	Dish	With flowers or rabbit	5″l	1940s–1960s
851	Basket	Wild Duck decoration	8½″l	1948–1950s
874	Twin Tray	Blackberry range, pink or primrose. Two triangles with blackberry in centre	10½″l	1949–1950s
876	Jugs	Blackberry range	Various sizes	1949–1950s
888	Honey	Leaf design	3½″h	1949–1950s
918	Biscuit	Barrel with lid	8″h	1940s–1950s
922	Holder	For candle or small posy	2″h 2½″dia	during 1950s
924	Vase/Bowl	Ribbed, yellow	3″dia 3″h	during 1950s
976	Ashtray	To commemorate the coronation of H.M. Queen Elizabeth 2nd	6¼″l	during 1950s
996	Basket	With dog, but also found with other animals	2″h	1950s–1960s
006	Jardiniere	Also with HP flowers	2″l 1½″h	1950s–1960s
062	Bowl	Tree stump with dogs	7¼″dia 3½″h	during 1950s
072	Jug	Ivyleaf range	6″h	during 1950s
073	Jug	Ivyleaf range	6″h	during 1950s

2074	Dish	Ivyleaf range	9¾"l	during 1950s
2078	Jug	Ivyleaf range	7¼"h	during 1950s
2092	Wall Vase	Chrysanthemum	9"h 7"dia	during 1950s
2093	Jug	Chrysanthemum		during 1950s
2097	Bowl	Chrysanthemum embossed	6"l 4"h	during 1950s
2144	Vase	Various decorations	11"h	1950s–1960s
2158	Pixie	Sitting on upturned toadstool	3¼"h	1950s–1960s
2177	Honey	Raphique range, assorted colours	4½"h	1950s–1960s
2198	Vase	Raphique range, assorted colours	5¼"h	during 1950s
2203	Teapot			during 1950s
2205	Vase	Fish standing on tail. Matt	7"h	during 1950s
2208	Wall Vase	With flowers	7"h	during 1950s
2212	Vase	Lace range	5½"h	during 1950s
2213	Jardiniere	Raphique range. Also seen in green matt	7"l	during 1950s
2235	Wall Vase	With circles, multi-coloured	7"h	during 1950s
2246	Vase	Cactus range	6"h	during 1950s
2261	Tray		6½"dia	during 1950s
2262	Wall Vase	Cactus range	6½"h	during 1950s
2267	Vase	Floral range, assorted colours	5¼"h	1950s–1960s
2332	Sock	Babies bootee, blue or pink	3¼"h	during 1950s
2333	Bowl	Nuleef range	10"l 6½"h	during 1950s
2343	Tankard	Horses head	4½"h	during 1950s
2353	Lettuce Dish	Nuleef range	11½"l	during 1950s
2404	Vase	Plume range	6¼"h	during 1950s
2406	Jardiniere	Plume range	8½"l 4"h	during 1950s
2420	Vase	Nuleef range with grid, assorted colours	8¼"h	during 1950s
2496 *	Dog	Springer Spaniel	7¼"h	
2498	Bowl	Also with seven HP flowers		1950s–1960s
2499	Bowl	Also with ten HP flowers		1950s–1960s
2505	Vase	Bulbous base narrowing in centre, two asymmetrical scrolls	15"h	1950s
2509	Barrel	Also with cat	2¼"h	1950s
2510	Bowl	Also with HP flowers		during 1950s
2525	Bowl	Also with fourteen HP flowers		during 1950s
2526	Bowl			during 1950s
2547	Posy	Bamboo range	3¾"h 5¾"l	during 1950s
2651	Vase	Ivy range, oval, two handles	10"l 7"h	during 1960s
2706	Vase	Looped design	8"h	during 1960s
2708	Jardiniere	Yellow	4½"h 6"dia	during 1960s
2711	Posy	Looped design	8"l	during 1960s
2712	Vase	Looped design	10"h	during 1960s
2713	Vase	Looped design	6"h	during 1960s
2758	Owl			during 1960s
2773	Vase	Lattice range	8½"h 5½"dia	during 1960s
2777	Vase	Bamboo design	6¼"h 4¼"dia	during 1960s
2801	Jardiniere	Lattice range	5½"h 3¾"dia	during 1960s
2803	Vase	On pedestal	6"h	during 1960s
2816	Jardiniere	Bamboo range scalloped rim	4¼"h 7¼"l 3¼"w	during 1960s
2817	Jardiniere	Lattice range, fan shape	6¾"l 3"w	during 1960s
2829	Holder	Probably for pens. With girl, boy, other or nothing	3¾"h	during 1960s
2831	Vase	Cone range	7"h	during 1960s
2846	Vase	Lumpy design, yellow	6½"h	during 1960s
2925	Jardiniere	Oak leaf design	11"dia	during 1960s
2927	Vase	Oak leaf design	8"h	during 1960s
2979	Vase	Embossed fern pattern	8"h	during 1960s
2991	Jardiniere	Oak leaf design	5"h	during 1960s
3023	Jardiniere	Fern pattern	8½"l 4"h	during 1960s
3092	Dog	Glum, sitting	4"h	during 1960s
3126	Dog	Lying. Griffon. Matt colours	4"h	during 1960s
3140	Elephant	Dumbo with big ears	5"l	during 1960s
3239	Elephant	With china flowers on its back	4¼"h	during 1960s
3265	Trough	Fuschia range	7¾"l	during 1960s
3269	Vase	Fuschia range	7¾"h	1960s–1982
3372	Tea Caddy	Known as the Sita Jar, with elephant head handles. Made for The Rington Tea Company, with lid	7½"h	1963
3376	Jardiniere	Deco style	5½"h 10½"l	during 1960s
3460	Vase	Seahorse	10"h	during 1960s
3465	Bowl	Opelle range	9½"l 9"w 2¾"h	during 1960s
3470	Posybar	Seahorse	8½"l	during 1960s
3475	Bowl	Seahorse	5"h 9½"l	during 1960s

3502	Twin Tray	Feather range	10″l 9″w	during 1960s
3529	Holder	New Shell Range	4¼″h 7½″l 5″w	during 1960s
3542	Ashtray	With Mr. SylvaC and dog with toothache, issued to retail outlets. Reproduced in 1989/90	8″h	1964 and 1989/90
3608	Bowl	Fluted. Seen in pink	3″h 6″dia	during 1960s
3665	Bowl	Pedestal	Medium size	during 1960s
3666	Bowl	Pedestal	Large Size	during 1960s
3667	Sugar Bowl	Pedestal		during 1960s
3668	Teapot	Pedestal		during 1960s
3669	Cream Jug	Pedestal		during 1960s
3684	Shell	For plant	6½″h	during 1960s
3694	Vase	Chequers pattern	8″h	during 1960s
3704	Planter/Trough		14½″l 3½″h	during 1960s
3710	Bowl	Palm	6½″l 4½″h	during 1960s
3720	Posy	Palm pattern	2⅜″h 8″l 2¼″w	during 1960s
3745	Sandwich Tray	Butterfly range	12½″l	during 1960s
3788	Egg Cup	Teddy Nursery range and Zooline. Also handpainted by E.F. Nelson with flowers in the style of Radford	3″dia	1960s–1989
3902	Posy Bar	Coral ware	9½″l	during 1960s
3927	Fox	Feeding chicken with axe behind its back	7″h	during 1960s
4111	Ashtray	Log	6″l	during 1960s
4168	Jardiniere	Flora range	12½″l	1960s
4198	Tray	Aurora, Evening Fantasy and Misty Morn ranges	7¼″l	1960s–1982
4254	Tankard	Misty Morn and other ranges	4⅝″h	1960s–1982
4288	Ashtray	With deer or squirrel, Woodland range	6″l	1960s–1970s
4497	Character Jug	Harrods Doorman. Mould sold to Carlton Ware and produced until 1989	4¼″h	1981
4546	Tray with Fox and Egg Cups	Fox has axe behind his back, and is attached to a tray with three chicken egg cups	5½″h 7¼″w	during 1960s
4553	Beetroot Bowl	With beetroot face	5″h	1969–1982
4757	Pot	Hoop. Six feet	5″h 5″dia	during 1960s
4849	Flower Holder	In shape of picture frame	6″h	during 1970s
4906	Holder	For pan scourer, beef stock or chicken stock. Later used for Fortnum and Mason's Finest English Blue Stilton Cheese	3¼″h	1971–1982+
4972	Ashtray	Specially commissioned for The Galloway Bull Society, has Bonnie Galloway on base, and is mounted with a Galloway Bull. Same base as 4288	6¼″l 3½″h	1972
5145	Ashtray	With Lesney Sand Buggy attached		1973
5146	Ashtray	With Lesney Aeroplane attached		1973
5167	Dog	Labrador standing. A small number were produced by mistake in green	9½″l	1974–1989
5207	Bull	Galloway medium size	4½″h 8″l	1974
5222	Tankard	With Indian Chief face for Benskins promotion	5¾″h	1981
5310	Ashtray	Plain. Oblong	7″l	1976
5451	Bowl	Powder Bowl for Anniversary range, also used as commemorative for the wedding of the Prince and Princess of Wales	4½″h	1978–1981

Always bear in mind when reading these numbers that many collectors have contributed to this information and although every effort has been made to eliminate errors the possibility always exists. Production dates have been gleaned from catalogues in my possession but new information can always alter what was thought to be correct. Sizes of items can vary slightly as the moulds are worn or replaced.

I have also found that descriptions of items have varied in the Mould Makers Register and also in different catalogues, which may account for varying descriptions in this book, but I have tried to be as consistent as possible.

◀ Early Shaw & Copestake mark used until about 1937.

Early SylvaC mark used from 1935 to about 1940. ▶

APPENDICES

APPENDIX A

IMPORTANT DATES IN THE HISTORY OF SHAW & COPESTAKE LIMITED

1894	Founding of the company by Mr. William Shaw and Mr. Copestake.
1898	Mr. Richard Hull senior joins the company replacing Mr. Copestake.
1902	First mention of the company in the Pottery Gazette under List of Manufacturers.
1904	First full page advert of Shaw & Copestake's products in the Pottery Gazette.
1924	Mr. Richard Hull junior joins the company at the age of 18.
1935	The demise of Mr. Richard Hull senior. Mr. Richard Hull junior becomes partner in the company with Mr. William Shaw.
1935	The SylvaC trade name is used for the first time.
1935	Participate in the British Industries Fair for the first time.
1936	A Limited Company is formed.
1938	Mr. Richard Hull and Mr. E.J. Dennis become directors of Thomas Lawrence (Longton) Ltd., Falcon Works, Waterloo Street, Longton, Stoke-on-Trent.
1939–1945	The Sylvan Works is requisitioned by the Government and used for storage. Shaw & Copestake move in with Thomas Lawrence (Longton) Ltd.
1942	Mr. William Shaw retires, and Mr. E.J. Dennis becomes a director of the company.
1947	Mr. E.J. Radford becomes a director of the company.
1950	The demise of Mr. William Shaw.
1953	Opening of the London Showrooms at 30 Brooke Street, Holborn.
1955	Start to build the new factory situated opposite the old works.
1957	The first piece of SylvaC made in the new kilns.
1957	Thomas Lawrence (Longton) Ltd., moves into the new premises. The old Falcon Pottery is sold to the John Beswick Company, now part of the Doulton Group.
1962	The new factory and office block is completed.
1962	Thomas Lawrence (Longton) Ltd., cease trading under their own name.
1962	Mr. Malcolm Chapman becomes a director of the company.
1964	Thomas Lawrence (Longton) Ltd., the company is finally wound up.
1966	Mr. George Matthews joins the company as a designer/modeller.
1974	The demise of Mr. E.J. Radford.
1974	Mr. E. Roy Taylor becomes Works Director.
1977	The demise of Mr. Richard Hull junior.
1978	Mr. Reginald Thompson, Chief Designer, retired after 62 years loyal service. He is awarded the British Empire Medal.
1982	Shaw & Copestake Ltd., go into voluntary liquidation.
1982	The Sylvan Works is purchased by the North Midlands Co-operative Society, and leased to a workers co-operative known as Longton Ceramics.
1983	United Co-operative Society, previously known as the North Midlands Co-operative Society take over the business which was run in the name of Crown Winsor.
1988	Mr. Reginald Thompson dies in April aged 85.
1988	The SylvaC Circle is formed by Mick and Derry Collins, and An Introduction to SylvaC published by them.
1989	June. The business is sold to Crown Winsor (Pottery) Ltd.
1989	August. The SylvaC Story is published, The History and Products of Shaw & Copestake. The book launch is held at the Sylvan Works. An exhibition of SylvaC at the Gladstone Pottery Museum until December 1989.
1989	November. Crown Winsor (Pottery) Ltd., go into receivership.
1989	December. The factory is finally closed.
1990	The premises are purchased by Portmeirion Potteries Ltd.
1991	The SylvaC Companion is published.

APPENDIX B

Sources and Bibliography

The Pottery Gazette and Glass Trade Review. Pottery and Glass, Tableware, and Tableware International. These publications can be seen at The City Museum and Art Gallery, Bethesda Street, Hanley, Stoke-on-Trent, and The Colindale Newspaper Library, Colindale Avenue, London NW9.

Encyclopaedia of British Pottery and Porcelain Marks by Geoffrey A. Godden, F.R.S.A. Published by Barrie and Jenkins Ltd, 289 Westbourne Grove, London W11 2QA. ISBN 0 257 65782 7.

The World of Wade by Ian Warner with Mike Posgay, published by Antique Publications, P.O. Box 553, Marietta, Ohio 45750, U.S.A. ISBN 0 915 410 50 8 and 0 915 410 51 6.

SylvaC and Falcon Works catalogues dating from 1936 to 1982.

Longton Ceramics Ltd., advertising leaflets.

Crown Winsor advertising leaflets.

Shaw & Copestake's Mould Makers Registers.

Mr. SylvaC introduces the housewife and SylvaC by Shaw & Copestake Ltd. Designed and produced at the Buxton Press.

SylvaC and its Manufacture by Shaw & Copestake Ltd.

SylvaC Ware Shape List by Shaw & Copestake Ltd.

SylvaC and Falcon Bulletin, Spring 1943 Vol. 1. No. 1.

SylvaC and Falcon Bulletin, Spring 1953 by Shaw & Copestake Ltd.

SylvaC and Falcon Bulletin – Production c.1950 by Shaw & Copestake Ltd.

Further Reading

An introduction to SylvaC by Mick and Derry Collins, published by The SylvaC Collectors Circle, 174 Portsmouth Road, Horndean, Hampshire. PO8 9HP. ISBN 0 9514202 0 8.

Shaw & Copestake, A Collectors Guide to Early SylvaC, by Anthony Van der Woerd, to be published Autumn 1991. Further information from Pottery Publications.

The SylvaC Story, The History and Products of Shaw & Copestake Ltd., by Susan Jean Verbeek, published by Pottery Publications, 7 Merton Park Parade, Kingston Road, London SW19 3NT. ISBN 0 9514889 0 2. £15.95 + £1.50 postage and packing.

Photo-copies of original SylvaC Catalogues are available from Pottery Publications, 7 Merton Park Parade, Kingston Road, London SW19 3NT. These are in slide binders with plastic covers. Send for list.

Miller's Collectables Price Guide 1990–1991 by Judith and Martin Miller, published by Millers Publications Limited, The Mitchell Beazley Group, Sissinghurst Court, Sissinghurst, Cranbrook, Kent TN17 2JA. ISBN 0 905879 58 9.

Bargain Antiques by Muriel Miller. (No further information available).

Other Interesting Publications

The Antiques Bulletin, H.P. Publishing, 226 Court Oak Road, Harborne, Birmingham B32 2EG. Telephone 021 427 9440. Available by post. Weekly publication.

The Antiques Trade Gazette, 17 Whitcomb Street, London WC2H 7PL. Telephone 071 930 7194. Available by post. Weekly publication.

Antique Collecting, The Journal of The Antique Collectors' Club, 5 Church Street, Woodbridge, Suffolk IP12 1DS. Telephone 0394 385501. Available by post. Monthly publication.

Collectors News, 11 Brook Lane, Felixstowe, Suffolk IP11 7EG. Telephone 0394 274550. A Bi-monthly publication published by collectors for collectors. Available by post or at all major Antique Fairs.

The World of Antiques, Philips Publishing, 10 Belvedere Road, Taunton, Somerset TA1 1BW. Telephone 0823 323562. A quarterly publication for connoisseurs and collectors. Available by post or at all major Antique Fairs.

Ashtead Potters Ltd., In Surrey 1923–1935, by Edward Hallam. The History and Products of the Ashtead Pottery. ISBN 0 9516007 0. £8.50 + £1.00 for postage and packing. Available from Pottery Publications.

The Shorter Connection by Irene and Gordon Hopwood. The History and Products of Shorter & Son Ltd., Stoke-on-Trent. To be published Autumn 1991. For further information telephone 0453 758328.

The Antique & Collectors Fayre, (No longer being published) Volume 3. No. 6 December 1988. Collecting SylvaC by Susan L'Epine-Smith erbeek) pages 18 and 19.

Antique Collecting, The Journal of The Antique Collectors' Club, Vol. 21 No. 5 October 1986. Collecting Wall Pockets by Pat Watson, ges 72 to 75.

Antique Collecting, The Journal of The Antique Collectors' Club, Vol. 21 No. 6 November 1986. A Sylvan Collection by Jeremy Thomas edman, pages 36 and 37.

Antique Collecting, The Journal of The Antique Collectors' Club, Vol. 24 No. 6 November 1989. A Guide to Collecting SylvaC by Susan erbeek, pages 48 – 51.

Collectors News, Issue 1 'Discovering SylvaC' by Mick and Derry Collins, pages 20 and 21.

The SylvaC Collectors Circle, Mick & Derry Collins, 174 Portsmouth Road, Horndean, Hampshire PO8 9HP. A Club Newsletter every ur months.

Although the above information is correct at the time of going to press, please bear in mind addresses and telephone numbers can change. stamped self addressed envelope would be appreciated when writing for information.

APPENDIX C

Antique Dealers, stocking SylvaC and some books

Cottage Curios,
39 High Street,
St. Peters,
Broadstairs,
Kent.

Antiques and collectables.

Please telephone for opening times
Telephone 0843 602806

Jimmy Cox,
Pot Luck Antiques,
Stoke-on-Trent.
Staffs.

Antiques and collectables.

Telephone 0782 335207

Edenbridge Antique Centre,
51 High Street,
Edenbridge,
Kent. TN8 5AL

Antiques and collectables.

Telephone 0732 862785

Sue Horrigan

20th Century collectables.
Telephone 081 558 1715
Attends all large London
Antique Fairs

London E10

J. Hulme
Charisma Collectables,
Stoke-on-Trent,
Staffs.

Antiques and collectables.

Telephone 0782 635534

Darrell Willis-Utting
Bay House,
Fallbarrow Road,
Bowness-on-Windermere,
Cumbria. LA23 3DJ

Collector, buyer, seller of
ANYTHING SylvaC!!

Telephone 09662 88662

Useful Information

Sandringham Fine Figurines,
36, Lower Mile House Lane,
Newcastle-under-Lyme,
Staffs. ST5 9AB

George Matthews, former SylvaC
modeller, makes figurines and wild
life models. Available at all good
China Shops.

The London Pottery Co., Ltd.,
96–98 Kingston Road,
Wimbledon,
London.
SW19 1LX

Specialists in designing food
containers. Retail outlet for novelty
teapots and unusual items. SylvaC
books stocked.
Telephone 081 543 2588

Portmeirion Potteries Ltd.,
Sylvan Works,
Normacot Road,
Longton,
Stoke-on-Trent,
Staffs.

Factory shop on premises.

Telephone 0782 313037 for
opening times.

Cottage Industry,
P.O. Box 38,
Ashford,
Middlesex. TW15 1QT

Supplier of tastefully designed
colour postcards depicting SylvaC.

Telephone 0784 242487

Falkland Promotions,
82A Falkland Road,
Dorking,
Surrey. RH4 3AD

Suppliers of special promotional
diecast models to Pottery
Publications.
Telephone 0306 880263

The Patent Office,
State House,
66–71 High Holborn,
London. WC1R 4TP

Trade Marks Registry.
Registered Pattern and Design
Numbers.
Telephone 071 831 2525

Public Records Office,
Ruskin Avenue,
Kew,
Surrey.

Also hold some Registered Pattern
and Design Numbers.

Telephone 081 876 3444

Meadows and Passmore,
Farningham Road,
Jarvis Brook,
Sussex. TN6 2JP

Suppliers of suitable clockwork and
battery movements for Shaw &
Copestake clocks. Four first class
stamps for general clock spares
catalogue.
Telephone 0892 662255

Book Sellers specialising in books on Collectables and Antiques, including The SylvaC Story and The SylvaC Companion.

Lionel Ringle,

London.

Specialises in books on Antiques
and Collectables.
Attends Fairs in the South East.
Telephone 081 202 9040

Lister Art Books,
Southport,
Lancs.

Importers, Distributors and
Booksellers. Orders and enquiries
welcome. Regularly attend the
Sunday Charnock Richard Fair.
Telephone 0704 541819 anytime.

The Museum Shop,
City Museum and Art Gallery,
Bethesda Street,
Hanley,
Stoke-on-Trent,
Staffs. ST1 3DW

Books on Pottery, Collectables etc.
Small exhibition of SylvaC in
Museum.

Telephone 0782 273173

C. & A.J. Barmby,
68 Judd Road,
Tonbridge,
Kent.

Reference books, trade accessories
display stands, plate stands and
wires etc., Mail Order. Callers by
appointment. Attends some
Antique Fairs.
Telephone 0732 356479

Graham Stead

Telephone 0732 452040

also at:

Tunbridge Wells Antiques Centre,
The Pantiles,
Tunbridge Wells,
Kent.

Antiques, Furniture and
Booksellers.
Telephone 0892 33708

also at:

The Antiques Centre,
London Road,
Sevenoaks,
Kent.

Antiques, Furniture and
Booksellers.
Telephone 0732 452104
Attends all the large Antique
Fairs and regular Sunday Fairs
at Ashford Hotel, Kent, and Great
Danes Hotel Nr. Maidstone, Kent.

Goss & Crested China Ltd.,
62 Murray Road,
Horndean,
Hants. PO8 9JL

Suppliers of books for and dealing
in Heraldic China, SylvaC, Carlton
Ware, Charlotte Rhead, and other
porcelain.
Telephone 0705 597440

Accommodation

ovelly Guest House,
 Uttoxeter Road,
ythe Bridge,
oke-on-Trent,
affs.

trigg Lodge Hotel,
ke Road,
eswick,
umbria. CA12 5DQ

Where the founder of Shaw &
Copestake, Mr. William Shaw used
to live.
Bed and Breakfast.
Telephone 0782 398958

SylvaC Collectors welcome. Full
board available and Restaurant.
Conveniently situated in a quiet,
traffic-free road a few minutes walk
from town centre and the Lake.
Telephone 07687 73545

Bay House Lake View
Guest House,
Fallbarrow Road,
Bowness-on-Windermere,
Cumbria. LA23 3DJ

Come for a break to the Heart of
the English Lakes. Reductions for
SylvaC fanatics (not during peak
season). Proprietors
Darrell & Nigel Willis-Utting.
Telephone 09662 3383

Before visiting any of the afore mentioned addresses it is advisable to
check the opening hours before starting off on your journey. Although all
the above information is correct at the time of going to press, addresses
and telephone numbers are frequently changed. If sending for information
it would be helpful to enclose a stamped self-addressed envelope.

FOOTNOTE

he following information was received from collectors too late to incorporate in the main text.

	Bread Plate	Old Shaw & Copestake 'Daisy' mark. Wavy edge. No number.	10¼" dia
)07	Vase	Plain shape. Decorated with Poppies and a village in the background	5" high
85	Butter dish	Round. Ribbed design	6" across
708	Bowl	Looped design	7¼" across
)70	Posy/Ashtray	Engraved 'With compliments of SylvaC'	4½ long
)86	Ashtray	Advertising SylvaC	6" across
554	Bootees	Pair of baby bootees cream with blue or pink trimming	3½" high
555	Stork	Carrying bundle. White with blue or pink trimming	4½" high

hank you to Mr. Patrick Boyle, Mrs. Valerie Fearis, Mr. Malcom Harris, for this last minute information.

▲ From the collection of John Howard. Photograph by Neil France.